AF521635

TEN PLAYS

DAVID PINSKI

TEN PLAYS

translated from the Yiddish by

ISAAC GOLDBERG

ONE-ACT PLAYS IN REPRINT

First Published 1920
Reprinted 1977

INTERNATIONAL STANDARD BOOK NUMBER
0-8486-2021-6

LIBRARY OF CONGRESS CATALOG NUMBER
77-70360

PRINTED IN THE UNITED STATES OF AMERICA

The original translation of " A Dollar " was made by Mr. Joseph Michael and of " Diplomacy " by Mr. Harry Birnbaum. These have been revised by Dr. Isaac Goldberg who translated the other eight plays.

Some of the plays first appeared in the New York Tribune and Boston Evening Transcript and two were included in a volume issued by John W. Luce & Co., to all of whom the author and publisher make due acknowledgment.

CONTENTS

THE PHONOGRAPH

A Comedy

PERSONS

NAHMEN RISKIN.
LIBBE, *his wife.*
HIS PARENTS.
HIS FATHER-IN-LAW AND MOTHER-IN-LAW.
TWO BROTHERS.
THREE BROTHERS-IN-LAW.
SISTERS, SISTERS-IN-LAW, AUNTS, *and so on.*
THE RABBI.
HIS WIFE.
THE WEALTHY MERCHANT.
HIS WIFE.
THE CANTOR.
HIS WIFE.
THE THIEF.
THE INFORMER.
THE TOWN IDIOT.

The action takes place in a remote Russo-Yiddish town, where the Jews lived upon wind and miracles.

THE PHONOGRAPH

THE SCENE: *A large room in the home of* NAHMEN RISKIN. *To the right, a door leading to the other rooms; to the left, the exit door; at the rear, two windows facing the street. In the middle of the room, a round table upon which there now reposes the phonograph, while overhead burns a hanging lamp. In the right foreground, a bureau; behind it, a closet; between the windows, a lounge; all manner of chairs and benches are placed in disarray; the room is packed with people. Some chairs hold two occupants; the benches creak under their excessive burden; even the bureau serves as a seat for some spectators; against the windowpanes curious faces are pressed, for a crowd has gathered outside.*

NAHMEN RISKIN (*in high feather, merrily relating something in the voice and manner of one who feels that he is the hero of the day and the center of universal admiration*). . . . So, as usual in America, they told me to become a tailor, like the rest of them. But just to spite them all, I said to myself: "No, you'll become no tailor. You've never held a needle in your fingers and you're not going to begin now, even if the world should turn upside down."

Libbe (*with disdain*). A tailor! Humph! The crazy notion!

Nahmen. So I threw myself into many things, sniffed and licked at this and that,— American business. . . . And once I happened to be sitting with our Brokhe — just as now, on a Saturday evening, and she has a phonograph, and the phonograph played, and suddenly I was struck by an idea. "You blockhead, you! Here you have a golden business! Why should you have to knock about America with a thousand trades and never a blessing? — Rather buy yourself such a hurdy-gurdy, take it back home with you and you've got a business from businessland.

The Mother. God's hand! To think that he should sail to America, and there should live our Brokhe, and she should have such a machine, and the machine should play, and he should be struck by the idea. . . . Ah, Lord of the universe, what a God we have in heaven!

Libbe. We needed some recompense, indeed, for all the troubles we have gone through.

Father-in-Law. Well, and when the idea struck you?

Mother-in-Law. Can't you see? So he went and bought one.

Nahmen. When the idea struck me I told no tales, but went off and bought a hurdy-gurdy and went to my people and said: "I'm going back home!"—"How? What? What do you mean?" —"Just what I say! Everybody comes to America to make money, and I intend to return home to make money."— So they all looked at me and laughed. "How do you expect to return home and make money, when you've come from there because you never were able to make ends meet?"— And they began to tell what I was in the old country, that all I was good for was to poke around with my cane and play chess and not know what to do with myself. So I laughed. "You'll soon be hearing big things of me," I told them. "You'll get the big news. All I needed was to make a short visit to America and catch on to the business methods. . . .

THE FATHER. Didn't you tell them anything about the machine?

NAHMEN. Do you take me for a fool? Do you think I was going to tell them, and have somebody rob me of my idea?

A SISTER. Were you afraid of Brokhe?

NAHMEN. If I told it to her, she'd tell it to somebody else, and somebody else would. . . .

MOTHER-IN-LAW. You acted very wisely.

LIBBE. Thank God. There are plenty of envious souls.

NAHMEN. And besides that, I had to be doubly careful. I had no government passport, so I had to steal across the border. . . .

A BROTHER-IN-LAW. And did you really steal across the border?

NAHMEN. Did I! It would take a thousand and one nights to tell the full story. What I had to suffer! Ah! It was hard enough at the time I went to America. On the way back it was a thousand times harder. A positive danger to life and limb. I was sure that I was going to lose both my phonograph and my life. But when a fellow carries a smart head on his shoulders, and doesn't lose his head, then everything is all right. . . .

An Uncle. How much does such a machine cost?

Nahmen. It costs a pretty sum of dollars. Would to God you earned it every week, or even every month.

A Second Uncle. Won't you have the kindness to let us hear another selection of that sweet synagogue music?

Nahmen. You'll hear it, in time. Too much is forbidden. The rabbi will soon come, and the merchant, and the cantor. Then you'll hear it. They ought to be here already. (*To those who are sitting upon the lounge.*) You will please leave the lounge when they arrive. Altogether, we'll have to have more room here. You can stand in the other rooms.

A Sister (*entreatingly*). Let "it" sing the same once again.

Nahmen. No-o-o. The first time, as a gift; the second time, you must pay.

A Brother. Surely you'll ask no money of us?

Nahmen. Certainly, of father and mother, father-in-law and mother-in-law. . . .

Mother-in-Law (*offended*). I might have expected you to ask me to pay.

Nahmen. Everybody must pay. That's business. Do you understand? Business. And in business there is no friendship. If I were to open a tavern would you expect me to give you free brandy? And if I were to open a grocery would you expect me to give you everything for nothing?

A Sister-in-Law. There's a comparison for you. If we hear your music, does that mean that we'll use up your machine?

Nahmen. What do you think, then? Certainly you would use it up. As it turns and turns around it uses up. And besides, this very listening you do, is my business. You pay for hearing.

The Mother-in-Law. Why should you play anything for the merchant without asking pay?

Nahmen. Well,— you see, he's a guest. And the rabbi will be here, as well as the cantor. And how much, do you think, am I going to play for him? One piece, another piece, and it's all over. And if he wishes some more, then he'll have to be so kind as to pay for it. And the rabbi, too, and the cantor likewise.

The Mother. What did you expect? That he shouldn't play for the rabbi and the merchant at all? It's such an honor.

Nahmen. Never mind the honor. I've been to America, remember. And over there they laugh at such matters. No matter how wealthy a man may be, and no matter how learned the rabbi may be, it makes no difference. But I'll tell the truth. I was anxious for the merchant to come so that he'd burst with envy. What do you think,— that his businesses are any better than mine?

LIBBE (*with a sudden outcry*). Oh, look who has come in! (*All eyes are focussed upon the doorway.*)

THE THIEF (*stands upon the threshold with a smile that reaches from ear to ear.*)

VOICES (*in fright*). The thief! The thief! (*The persons seated around the table jump to their feet and conceal the phonograph from the intruder's sight.*)

THE THIEF. Aren't you ashamed to call a man a thief before his very face? So inconsiderate of you! I might take offence, ha-ha-ha! And why did you get so scared? I'm not going to steal your pretty little American from you. (*Steps into the room. The guests recoil and open up passage for him.*)

THE MOTHER. May your hands wither if you dare to lay them upon the little American. If you come a step nearer, I'll scratch your eyes out for you.

THE THIEF. Hush, sh. . . . I'm not stealing anything.

VOICES. Really. . . . That's so. . . . Why insult him? . . . He's not stealing anything. . . .

NAHMEN (*recovers from his fright, and suddenly recalls that he is something of an American and that the room is full of men, whose count he has just been taking*). What do you wish here?

THE THIEF. What should I wish? Just a mere look. The whole town has come for a look, so I'm here, too.

NAHMEN. You've no business coming into my home, so clear out of here at once! (*Some of the guests are frightened at* NAHMEN'S *resolute manner and tug at his coat to warn him that it is more tactful to treat a thief in kind and friendly fashion.*)

A BROTHER-IN-LAW. Let him have a look. What do you care?

ANOTHER. Simply let him keep his hands off. He can't hurt anything with his eyes.

THE THIEF. As long as you see me, there's nothing to fear. You need be afraid only when you *don't* see me. When you retire, and put out the lights, and fall asleep. . . . Ha, ha, ha. . . .

NAHMEN. And I tell you to get out of here at once. I come from America, I'll have you understand. And in America folks know what a revolver is. Do you wish to see it, perhaps? Clear out on the instant!

THE THIEF. Just look at the airs he's putting on. The cock of the walk! A revolver and such things. . . . With a thief, it seems to me, it is better to be on good terms. It's wise to make him the keeper of your keys, ha, ha, ha. . . . (*Tries to catch a glimpse of the phonograph.*)

NAHMEN (*thrusts him aside*). You'd better go out before I throw you out!

THE THIEF. Ha, ha, ha! . . . Rather be so kind as to present me with a little music. Have that kindness, and I'll leave.

VOICES. Oh! Yes! Really!

NAHMEN. I'll soon play him a tune that'll. . . .

The Thief. Do you know what? I'll pay you with the small change I've picked from the pockets of the crowd that's assembled before your windows. Ha, ha, ha! . . . (*He jingles the change in his pocket. Some of the hearers take the* Thief's *words for a jest, and laugh; others thrust their hands hastily into their pockets.*)

The Mother. His hands should have been paralyzed!

The Mother-in-Law. We ought to send for the police.

The Thief (*boastfully, and content with the impression he has made*). Would you accept a nice little watch? It's worth a couple of rubles. Not much. Your crowd is composed of paupers! And with Sabbath pockets. Fumble and fumble and there's nothing to get out of them. Sabbath cigarettes, hidden away, unsmoked, and other like treasures. . . .

A Brother. Really, take his small change and play him a tune.

The Father. Stolen money!

Libbe. We don't need his thefts.

Nahmen. I'll see to it that he leaves in a moment. Just keep him away from the table. (*Hastens through the door at the right.*)

The Thief (*somewhat intimidated, draws back*). He refuses to believe that I simply wish to hear. How is it possible, really, to steal the little American lady? Why, if you just touch her, she's liable to let out a shriek and commence to scream, ha, ha, ha!

. . . He thinks he'll scare me. . . . I'll give him just one daub and he'll be lying at my feet, yelping like a whipped cur. . . . What are you all looking at me like that for? . . . That's the way! Tremble! Then you'll let me have a glimpse of the American lady. (*Draws closer to the table.*)

NAHMEN (*returns*).

THE THIEF (*steps back, staring at* NAHMEN'S *fingers. Seeing that the latter has returned with empty hands, he bursts into laughter.*) With what he went out, he returns. Ha, ha, ha! (*Approaches the table once more.*)

NAHMEN (*with his eyes directed upon the table, advances at the same time toward the thief, and as he draws very near he suddenly delivers a resounding slap, nearly knocking the fellow off his feet; at once he whips out a revolver from his back pocket and levels it at the thief*). Now get right out, or you'll be carried out a corpse!

THE THIEF (*lost, terrified, he edges his way to the door and dashes out, followed by* NAHMEN *and some of the bystanders*).

THE CROWD (*at first amazed, breathless and speechless, finally explodes into laughter*).

A VOICE. That was a slap!

A SECOND VOICE. And the revolver under his nose!

A THIRD. And off with you!

A WOMAN. Oh, I shivered all over. I thought he was going to shoot.

NAHMEN (*returns*). We're rid of him for good. (*The crowd holds its sides for laughter.*)

AN UNCLE. And would you really have shot him?

NAHMEN. Bah! An empty revolver! Not loaded!

A BROTHER-IN-LAW. No bullets in it?

NAHMEN. What do you think? I wouldn't hold a loaded revolver. Why, a loaded revolver might actually shoot.

LIBBE. Just the same I'd advise you not to hold it.

NAHMEN. This is what you call a real revolver. You can put six bullets into it. I said to myself, "I've got to steal over the border line, and I must be able to protect my baggage, so it pays to have a shooter around." And it occurred to me, too, that it could be of use here. I actually expected thievish visitors. . . .

THE MOTHER. Fie! Hide it. I can't bear the sight of it.

NAHMEN (*places the weapon in his pocket*).

THE MOTHER-IN-LAW. See! He's putting it into his pocket!

NAHMEN. But it's empty. Didn't you hear what I was just saying?

A BROTHER. A good thing the thief didn't know that.

SECOND BROTHER. That slap alone was enough to send him scampering to where pepper grows.

THE FATHER-IN-LAW. Where did you learn to slap like that?

The Father. From me, of course! Many's the slap I've given him!

Nahmen (*caressing the phonograph*). I've gone through quite a bit for the sake of this fellow. He'll have to pay me back well. He'll have to become a good business for me.

A Sister-in-Law. Do you know what I'll tell you? Let us celebrate the exit of the thief. Wind up your machine and give us a tune.

Voices. Yes, yes!

A Second Sister-in-Law. The other people, perhaps, won't show up.

Nahmen. Well, if they don't come, we'll go to sleep.

An Aunt. Hush. I'll pay my share. How much do you ask?

Voices. We'll pay, too.

Nahmen. Fine. Out with your coins, then. . . . Business is business. Ten kopeks apiece. And then we'll have music. (*He puts out his hand and several of ihe guests throw coins into it.*)

The Informer (*enters*). Good week to you.

Nahmen (*turns and notices him, quivering with fright*).

Libbe (*looks at* Nahmen, *sees that he is perturbed, whereupon she is infected with his fright and wrings her hands*).

The Informer. Won't anybody answer my greeting with a " Good year to you "?

The Mother. Nobody sent for you.

THE MOTHER-IN-LAW. Informers are greeted with: "Go to the deuce!"

THE INFORMER. I never informed against you, did I? (*Approaching* NAHMEN.) Welcome, Mr. Riskin! (*Offers his hand.*)

NAHMEN (*gives him his hand*). The same to you.

THE INFORMER. You see, he isn't afraid of me. He knows I have nothing to inform about, against him. And he doesn't take offence for other people's wrongs.— So that's the machine, is it?—A little box.— Has it played already? May I hear something, too?

THE MOTHER (*scornfully*). Yes! Play something in *his* honor!

A BROTHER-IN-LAW. Maybe you've got a song there called, "A curse on you, Informer!" (*Laughter.*)

NAHMEN (*cordially*). We are waiting for the rabbi, the merchant and the cantor to arrive. When they come we'll play the machine and you, too, will hear.

THE INFORMER. Then we'll wait. I'm not so important a personage as they, yet I'll enjoy their good fortune.

NAHMEN (*almost apologetically*). To play the phonograph too often isn't good for its health.

THE INFORMER. Very well. I'm in no hurry. I'll wait.— Tell me, pray, what kind of voyage did you have?

NAHMEN. Excellent. How should it be? I

sailed on a first-class vessel. A speedy liner. Travelled second-class, like a lord,— like a real American.

THE INFORMER. But you must have had your troubles at the border.

NAHMEN. What do you mean? Why? Just the opposite, in fact.

THE INFORMER. What do you mean, " the opposite "? When a man crosses the border with an American machine and without a passport. . . .

NAHMEN. Without a passport? What do you mean, without a passport? May we all have a fortune as surely as I had a passport.

THE INFORMER. A — false one?

NAHMEN. Ah, you wish to insult me? What do you mean by " a false one "? Don't you know that I sailed for America with a government passport?

THE INFORMER. I know that you sailed for America *without* a government passport. I know even what you wrote about how you stole across the border.

NAHMEN (*laughing*). Cross yourself; you probably heard that about somebody else.

THE MOTHER-IN-LAW. What's this? Are you getting ready to inform against him?

NAHMEN (*angrily*). Inform! What has he to inform about? The police know that I had a passport.

THE INFORMER. And so is the machine not contraband? You paid duty on it?

NAHMEN. Eleven rubles and forty-nine kopeks, just as truly as it's Saturday night upon earth. Why, I have the receipt.

THE INFORMER. Then you're an innocent man, after all.

NAHMEN. Might the same be said of every Jewish soul!

THE INFORMER. Then I can't earn anything here.

NAHMEN. An American cigarette. (*Offers him the cigarette case.*)

THE INFORMER. Well, we'll take what we can get. Let's see how an American cigarette tastes. Although, for crossing the border without a passport, and smuggling in a phonograph. . . .

NAHMEN. If that were true, it would really be a bad state of affairs.

THE INFORMER. Just the same, I believe that a little informing wouldn't be a bad thing. . . . (*A stir in the crowd.*) Just see how they all started!— I, you will understand, take intense pleasure in informing. I gain weight on it. Ha, ha. . . . And on the contrary, if I should ever let slip an opportunity to inform, I'd be liable to get sick with heartache. As if I lost who knows what. Like a pious Jew who omits a prayer. That's the kind of informer I am. And it's entirely possible that I should inform against you for the pure pleasure of the thing. It may be that you really had a passport, that you paid duty upon the machine and have a receipt, but in the meantime the police would come, would make an investigation, and there'd be a hubbub and I'd have had my little joke, ha, ha, ha! Well, why are you all so frightened? If you wish, I can restrain my desire to inform. It can do me harm, but I am willing to risk my health if there's enough in it.

Nahmen. What, for instance?

Informer. Take me in as a partner.

Voices. Did you hear what he asks? — Oh, a plague upon him! —

Nahmen. Do you know what I'm going to do to you?

Informer. What, for example?

Nahmen. What I did to the thief. I gave him a punch in the jaw and almost shot him.

Informer. Oho, if that's the case, then I'll certainly do right to inform against you. (*Arises.*)

Nahmen (*pointing the revolver at him*). You'll not leave this room alive.

Crowd (*at first takes fright at sight of the revolver; then the various bystanders begin to choke back their laughter*).

Informer (*tries to escape*).

Nahmen (*holding him*). You can't run away. You're going to sit down and write a little letter for me. (*Sits the* Informer *down upon a chair. To his wife.*) Libbe, bring paper, ink and pen.

Libbe (*goes into the next room to get the materials*).

Nahmen. You are to write down that you heard I had come from America with a great deal of money and you offer to sell me counterfeit bills. Now you understand, if you dare to inform against me, your letter will be delivered into the hands of the police. The most they can do to me if I have paid no duty, is to take away my phonograph; but you will languish in prison.

INFORMER. How am I to write such a letter for you? Suppose I don't inform against you, and you take it into your head to give my letter to the police anyway?

NAHMEN. You write that letter like a good little boy, and ask questions afterwards, unless you wish to leave this place lame with an ear shot off.

INFORMER. You certainly learned a thing or two in America. Do you know what? Let's become partners in informing!

LIBBE (*enters with writing materials*).

NAHMEN. I'll soon make you a partner with the angel of death. Write down what I've told you to.

INFORMER. To think that I should fall into this! I should have had the additional pleasure of informing the authorities that you carried a revolver. You'll see, I'll fall ill because of all this. If I should die, remember that it was you who shortened my years.

THE MOTHER-IN-LAW. May it happen as soon as possible.

VOICES. Amen!

VOICES (*from outside*). The rabbi is coming! — The cantor is coming! — Here comes the merchant!

NAHMEN (*to the* INFORMER). Write, at once!

INFORMER. The pen can't move! My hand can't stir!

NAHMEN. Shall I shoot you? You can't get out of this, I tell you. (*To his* BROTHERS *and* BROTHERS-IN-LAW.) Do you know what? You fellows will be so kind as to take this chap into the bedroom, until the guests leave. The five of you should be able to keep a close watch over him. You may tie him to the bedpost, if you care to.

INFORMER. I'll raise an outcry, and you'll see what will happen.

NAHMEN. Then I'll shoot off your nose. Better do as you're told, without any resistance.

A BROTHER. But we wish to hear the phonograph.

NAHMEN. You can hear it from there. . . . And I'll give you a separate concert . . . later.

A BROTHER-IN-LAW. Then give me back my ten kopeks.

NAHMEN. How? What? Oh, yes. Here's your ten kopeks — and off with you! (*To the* INFORMER.) Move, now! One, two, three. . . .

A BROTHER (*to the* INFORMER.) Come, my good sir, we'll keep a watchful eye on you. (*The five men leave with him, going into the next room; they are followed by general laughter.*)

A SISTER-IN-LAW. Do you see what America makes of a man?

A SECOND SISTER-IN-LAW. An expert shooter. (*The guests appear; the* RABBI *and his wife, the* MERCHANT *and his wife, the* CANTOR *and his wife. They greet all with a "Good week!" and from all sides comes the response, "Good week! Good year!")*

NAHMEN (*to the previous visitors*). Will all of you please go into the other rooms. You can hear from there. Then we'll have more room in here. And more air. (*The people walk out most unwillingly. There remain only* NAHMEN'S *father and mother, his father-in-law and mother-in-law and a few elderly folk.*)

THE RABBI. You won't be offended that I've brought my wife along?

THE RABBI'S WIFE. I said to him: Why shouldn't I have the pleasure?

THE MERCHANT. I did the same thing myself. Without asking your permission.

THE MERCHANT'S WIFE. I said to him: Don't worry. They won't drive me out.

THE CANTOR'S WIFE. And *I* said: How will they do without an expert in music, like myself?

NAHMEN. You are all welcome, I assure you. Let me introduce my wife. Mrs. Riskin, as the Americans say, ha, ha, ha. . . . My father, my mother. . . .

RABBI. Yes, yes, we know them. . . . So that's the machine? That box there? (*They group themselves around the table and feel the phonograph with amazement.*)

CANTOR. And this box here sings like a cantor and his choir, and speaks Hebrew?

RABBI'S WIFE. I thought it was some sort of huge box, and that the cantor and his choir got inside. . . .

NAHMEN (*he has placed a record upon the revolving disc*). The cantor in the box will now sing "Lay us down," accompanied by his choir.

CANTOR. "Lay us down in peace"? Whose composition? Pitshe, the cantor's? (*The phonograph begins to play. No sooner have the first sounds issued from the machine than the guests almost cry in astonishment.*)

CANTOR. It's really "Lay us down." Wait! Pitshe's? Sulzer's? The Belzer's?

CANTOR'S WIFE. Oh, dear me! Just listen to that! A choir! And a real cantor!

MERCHANT'S WIFE. Why, the thing is really praying!

RABBI (*piously*). Blessed be the Lord that He has preserved us unto this day, to witness this miracle. (*Smacks his lips with pleasure and fervor.*)

RABBI'S WIFE (*begins to peep under the table, as if seeking some concealed persons, and then eyes* NAHMEN *with a penetrating glance, to see whether the tones are not coming from him.*)

CANTOR (*delighted, begins to sway piously to and fro, chiming in with the music between his exclamations*). Ay, ay, ay! . . . "And succor us." . . .

MERCHANT. Hush!

CANTOR (*bites his under lip, shuts his eyes, sways and sways to and fro, marking time with his right index finger. At last he cannot restrain an outburst of admiration and enthusiasm*). Ay, ay, ay! . . .

CANTOR'S WIFE (*places her hand over his mouth,*

but he does not cease to sway, until the record comes to its end. Then he opens his eyes).

CANTOR. Ay, ay, ay. . . . As far as the cantor is concerned,— well, we'll let that pass. I've heard plenty of them in my day. . . . I heard Pitshe himself. . . . I myself, if I only had a few of those upper notes, and also a few of those lower notes. . . .

CANTOR'S WIFE. And a few of the middle ones and a few of those between the upper ones and the middle ones and between the middle ones and the lower ones. . . .

MERCHANT. Oh, I guess that when the Holy Days come around again, we'll rather put this phonograph before the altar, instead of the cantor.

CANTOR. And suppose that fellow inside there sang without his hat on?

RABBI. Wonder of wonders! I can't find words. There stands a box, and out of the box issues a voice, a chorus of voices, a cantor and his choir, and chants a prayer, in really excellent Hebrew,— pure Hebrew! Miracles! A miracle of creation!

RABBI'S WIFE. I've been looking under the table. I shouldn't be surprised if somebody were concealed there.

THE MOTHER-IN-LAW. God befriend you! What are you talking about, good woman?

NAHMEN (*after having put on another record*). Now you're going to hear another prayer. So sweet that it simply turns your head. (*The phonograph begins to play. Suddenly a cry arises from without, growing to a tumult.*)

LIBBE. Oh! What can that be?

NAHMEN (*seizes the phonograph and carries it into another room*).

THE TOWN IDIOT (*comes dashing into the house*). I'm a funnygraf, too! I'm a funnygraf! (*Goes through the motions of winding himself up and commences to sing in wild tones.*)

NAHMEN (*returns, and with the aid of a few others throws the* IDIOT *out*).

MERCHANT'S WIFE. I am so scared!

LIBBE. I'm trembling from head to foot.

MERCHANT. And meanwhile the music was cut short.

CANTOR. Ay, ay, ay! . . .

RABBI. Wonder of wonders!

CANTOR'S WIFE. Can you bring the cantor in the box back now?

NAHMEN. No more. It's closed now, for good. It isn't so easy to open it. And it's time to clear the crowd away from the windows. (*Opens a window and calls to the crowd.*) You can break up now. There'll be no more singing. It's been closed. (*He closes the window, and from outside comes the bustle, noise and laughter of a crowd that gradually disappears. Some of the visitors begin to leave, too, wishing a "good year" as they go.*)

RABBI. Thanks for the entertainment. (*Arising.*) And if you should invite me again, I'll certainly thank you.

RABBI'S WIFE (*approaching the table and looking underneath*). I simply can't get it out of my head that. . . . Maybe Reb Nahmen is a ventriloquist? (*Laughter.*) There *are* such people, you know. . . .

CANTOR. I've got a good mind to learn those pieces. Too bad we didn't hear the whole of the second selection. I'll have to hear it over and over again. The cantor isn't so much, but the choir, the choir! If I only had such a choir, and those upper notes. . . .

CANTOR'S WIFE. Ah, ah! If I only had that box for a husband!

RABBI. You've already told us at the synagogue how our fellow Jews live in America. I'd certainly be glad to hear more and more. But you must be weary from the journey. You arrived yesterday evening, and I guess you've been talking aplenty since then. And I've got a great deal to do myself, tonight. Tomorrow, after prayers, if you'll have the time, you'll please remind me that I wished to ask you something.

NAHMEN (*somewhat impatient*). Surely. Surely.

RABBI. A good week to you.

RABBI'S WIFE. A good week to you and many thanks. There isn't any witchcraft about all this, is there, Reb Nahmen? I mean to say. . . . You know. . . . What can't folks do with witchcraft?

RABBI. But witchcraft wouldn't say prayers.

CANTOR'S WIFE. Let it be witchcraft, so long as it's beautiful. Good week to you.

CANTOR. Ay, ay, ay! Ah! Na! Well, good week to you. (*The* CANTOR *and his wife leave.*)

MERCHANT. And I'm not going yet, because I have something to talk over with you.

NAHMEN (*impatient, casting a glance in the direction of the door behind which the* INFORMER *is held captive*).

MERCHANT. Business. And I don't like to postpone business matters.

NAHMEN. Just a minute. I must tell my brothers something. They are in the next room. (NAHMEN *goes out.*)

MERCHANT. There's business in America! Every man ought to take a trip to America. That's where you can learn a thing or two and make rapid strides. Ah, America! The greatest millionaires! And everything's reckoned in dollars! Do you realize what that means? If a man has a million over there, it's like two million over here! Do you see the vast difference? If I have a hundred rubles in my pocket now, and go to America, it becomes fifty — do you see that difference? I become a poor man. And on the contrary, if I have a hundred dollars in my pocket and come from there to here, I have two hundred rubles. Do you understand what it means? Ay, America!

NAHMEN (*enters, closing the door behind him*). To tell the truth, I'm feeling very tired. . . .

MERCHANT. If you refuse to talk business merely because you're tired, then you're no business man. An American business man is certainly never tired.

NAHMEN. That's just what I was about to say.

To tell the truth, I *am* quite tired — I returned only yesterday, after a hard voyage. But since it's a matter of business, there must be no delay. Only remember that I believe in the American way: a word, a nod — done.

MERCHANT. But it doesn't seem to me that in America they do business before a roomful of people.

MOTHER-IN-LAW. That means us, I presume.

FATHER-IN-LAW. Then let's be off. (*The* FATHER *and* MOTHER, *the* FATHER-IN-LAW *and the* MOTHER-IN-LAW, *and the other guests, rise, exchange wishes for a good week, and leave. The wives of the five men who are guarding the* INFORMER *go to their husbands.* LIBBE *sits down beside the* MERCHANT'S WIFE.)

MERCHANT. I have no objection to our wives remaining here.

NAHMEN (*nervous; takes out a cigarette, lights it, and is about to replace his cigarette-case when he bethinks himself, and offers it to the* MERCHANT). Do you smoke?

MERCHANT. What's the sense of smoking? It's money thrown out.— Well, tell me just what you intend to do with your machine.

NAHMEN. Business, of course.

MERCHANT. Very well; but just how?

NAHMEN. Just like that.

MERCHANT. What do you mean: "just like that"?

NAHMEN. I have brought a machine that sings and plays — gives concerts. And there is a public here that's fond of singing and playing — is fond of concerts. That makes us a good match.

MERCHANT. True. True. So, from the way it seems, you'll hire a store, and set up a sort of theatre. . . .

NAHMEN. I'll see to the details later.

MERCHANT. And you'll remain in this town all the time?

NAHMEN. Maybe I'll pay visits to the surrounding towns, where there are no phonographs.

MERCHANT. Hm! Go on the road, too. That's what I thought. Travel, too. When the market grows dull here, and the people have had their fill, you'll go "on the road," and when you return, the folks here will be ready for more. Isn't that so?

NAHMEN. That's how I look at it.

MERCHANT. Then we agree.

NAHMEN. But what business did you want to speak of?

MERCHANT. That's exactly to what we are coming now. Just why is your business a business, or as you put it,— a match? Because you have the machine that sings, and the public likes singing. But suppose there is another machine hereabouts, and yet another? The match begins to get a bit shaky, and the business is spoiled. And if these other machines should get ahead of you in the other towns, then the business is certainly ruined. Do you understand?

NAHMEN. I can't see what you're driving at.— Are you going to order other machines?

MERCHANT. Well, well! You have a smart head on your shoulders!

LIBBE (*groans*).

NAHMEN. Then why need you tell me all this?

MERCHANT. Because I'm an honest man. Instead of becoming your competitor, I prefer to become your partner.

NAHMEN. Partner? What do I need a partner for?

MERCHANT. Then I'll be your competitor. What do you need a competitor for? — How much do you expect to ask for admission?

NAHMEN. How much? Twenty kopeks.— Twenty-five kopeks. Children, ten kopeks.

MERCHANT. And your competitor can make the fee cheaper. You know yourself, I have a store in my own building. I won't have to pay any rent. . . .

NAHMEN. And what are your terms of partnership?

MERCHANT. We'll divide the profits.

NAHMEN. How much money will you invest in the business?

MERCHANT. Invest money? What do you need money for? To put in chairs? To pay rent? You'd have to do that anyway.

NAHMEN. Then what sort of partner are you?

MERCHANT. My partnership will consist in my not being a competitor.

NAHMEN. And for that you ask half the profits?

MERCHANT. Naturally. If I should become your competitor, you'd be lucky to make the half that you'll have under the terms of our partnership.

NAHMEN. Hmmm. . . .

MERCHANT. You'll rent the store from me. I'll let you have it very cheap. Cheaper than it was.

NAHMEN. And suppose I don't care to?

MERCHANT. Then I'll send for several machines.

LIBBE. You've got enough business of your own, I should think!

MERCHANT. There's no such thing as enough in business. Now your husband knows how they do in America.

LIBBE. But *this* business wasn't your idea.

MERCHANT. And do you think that I thought out my other business ventures? Who cares about *who* thought it out. Business is business. As soon as a new business appears, it becomes public property. Whoever has the money, may engage in it.

LIBBE. But to snatch the food out of another man's mouth!

MERCHANT. Business! And suppose he takes it into his head to steal *my* business? Maybe he can run it better than I can. For he's an American, recollect.

A BROTHER (*enters*). See here. This has got to end sometime. We can't stay in there all night. . . .

NAHMEN. Come in, all of you.

BROTHER. All? Shall we bring *him* in, too?

NAHMEN. Surely. (*Calls into the next room.*) Come in, all of you! Bring him in, too!

MERCHANT. Whom shall they bring in? The phonograph?

MERCHANT'S WIFE (*uneasy*). I think it would be better if we went home. (*The guards and their wives enter with the* INFORMER.)

MERCHANT. He? What has this fellow been doing here?

NAHMEN. He wished to become my partner, too.

MERCHANT. He?

NAHMEN. Why not? And if I wasn't willing, he threatened to inform against me.

MERCHANT. A dangerous fellow. We'll have to attend to him —

NAHMEN. I've done that already. You'll see at once how he writes me out a document that'll make him hold his tongue. (*Takes out his revolver.*) Sit down, my fine fellow, and write! (*At sight of the revolver the* MERCHANT'S WIFE *recoils in fright; the* MERCHANT, *too, is uneasy; the guards, without any too great tenderness, seat the* INFORMER *and force the pen in between his fingers.*) And see that your fingers fly this time, or I'll see to it that you have a few less. You know already what you're supposed to write. You offer me counterfeit bills. (*To the guards.*) Watch what he writes. So that he won't have to do it over again. I've got something else to attend to now. (*Pointing the weapon at the* MERCHANT.) You're going to sit down and write something for me, too.

MERCHANT'S WIFE. Oh! My God! Oh! I'll raise an outcry! . . .

NAHMEN. If you dare, I'll shoot you. Understand; I'm an American. You heard your own husband say so.

MERCHANT (*bewildered*). What shall I write?

NAHMEN. First sit down where you were before. Right here at the table. Libbe, let's have another pen.

LIBBE (*exit*).

NAHMEN (*to the* MERCHANT'S WIFE). And you sit down, too, where you sat before. And be quiet. Not a chirp from you, remember. Do you see these six holes in the revolver? These are for six bullets. Do you understand what that means?

MERCHANT'S WIFE. Oh, I'm ready to faint. Oh, I'll soon take one of my shrieking fits! . . .

NAHMEN. Faint, if you must. But none of your shrieking fits. Sit still, there. As soon as he writes out his paper, you may go home in peace. (*To the* INFORMER.) And you stop looking in this direction. Finish your writing!

LIBBE (*enters with a pen*).

NAHMEN (*giving the pen to the* MERCHANT *and handing him a sheet of paper*). Write down that if another phonograph should appear in this town you must give me five thousand rubles.

MERCHANT. Even if the machines are not ordered by me?

NAHMEN. Even if not ordered by you. And none of your chaffering. Write as I tell you. And as a wise precaution, you'll write me a note for five thousand rubles.

MERCHANT. I'll write no notes; under no circumstances.

NAHMEN (*bringing the weapon close to the* MERCHANT'S *face*). You won't, ha?

MERCHANT'S WIFE. Oy, oy, oy! . . .

NAHMEN. Hush, there! (*To a* BROTHER.) Go, Layzer, and fetch us a note somewhere.

BROTHER. Where can I get one now?

NAHMEN. From hell itself, if you must. Hurry. You'll surely get one at Hirshe the money lender's.

BROTHER (*exit*).

MERCHANT. But this is highway robbery.

NAHMEN. Write and keep your mouth shut. We'll discuss robbery later.

INFORMER (*to the* MERCHANT). We can both learn our business from him.

NAHMEN. Finish your writing!

INFORMER. I've finished already. All I need do is sign my name. Such an outrage.

NAHMEN. So. Now let's have what you've written. (*Takes the document from the* INFORMER. *To the* MERCHANT.) Sit still, there. Don't dare to stir. (*Takes the paper from him likewise.*) Now all you have to do is write out a note.

INFORMER. May I go now?

NAHMEN. Wait till I read this through. Then you can go to hell for all I care. (*He scans both documents.*) Fine. Excellent. (*Giving them to* LIBBE.) Fold them and place them here in my inside pocket. Libbe, I'm going to become a great business man. I didn't realize myself what was in me. Do you hear? I'm a different person entirely, it seems. How shall I put it? I seem to have grown up. . . . I seem. . . .

Brother (*running into the house*). The police are coming! (*Intense amazement.*)

Informer. And *I* not the informer! Disgusting!

CURTAIN

THE GOD OF THE NEWLY RICH WOOL MERCHANT

PERSONS

The Newly Rich Wool Merchant.
His Wife.
His Son.
His Mother.
The Organist.
The Butler.
An Usher.
A Doctor.
Guests, Ushers, Servants, Etc.

THE GOD OF THE NEWLY RICH WOOL MERCHANT

SCENE: *A vast, temple-like hall in the home of the* WOOL MERCHANT, *illuminated by countless electric lights upon the ceiling and the walls. Floor, ceiling and walls are alike covered with wool, the floor with earth colored wool, the walls with wool of bright rose hue, the ceiling sky blue. At the rear a Holy Ark, bedecked with purple-red wool; the Ark is approached by several steps that lead to a broad altar platform. The curtains of the Ark are of white wool and are adorned with purple-red woollen David's shields (six-cornered stars). Above the Holy Ark are the pipes of a huge organ, enveloped in white wool. A broad strip of green wool extends entirely across the middle of the stage, leading also from the doors to the steps before the Holy Ark and covering also the steps and the altar. On both sides of the Holy Ark, placed perpendicularly to the rear wall and reaching to the central green strip, rows of benches; each bench can hold four persons and is covered with dark blue wool. Two doors at the right and left respectively are similarly covered with dark blue wool. The* WOOL MERCHANT, *a man of middle age with a flourishing white beard, and the* ORGANIST, *gray and clean shaven, are discovered standing not far from the door to the right, engrossed in conversation.*

THE WOOL MERCHANT. Yes, indeed. You have succeeded admirably, I must admit. The truth is the truth. Your music serves my purpose splendidly. It is suited to prayer as well as to dancing. Don't I seem crazy to you with all my dancing? Don't I appear foolish to you?

ORGANIST. H'm! Indeed! Why? I understand you perfectly. The ancient Greeks danced, too, when they worshipped their gods.

MERCHANT. King David, too, danced before the ark. When you feel God very close to you, you wish to serve him with every limb. So you have to dance. Naturally, I don't do it so well yet. Of course, an experienced dancer would do it far better, far more gracefully. You will be so kind as to play over for me your finale — from that point where the dance grows faster and more ardent. You know — trala, la, la, la. . . . Will you have the kindness?

ORGANIST. With pleasure!

MERCHANT. I want to have just one more little rehearsal — to dance through that finale just once more.

ORGANIST (*bows and leaves through the door at the right*).

MERCHANT (*raises his arms and begins to make pious dance gestures, rolling his eyes and closing them. At first his movements are slow, then they become livelier. The organ commences to play. The tune is a fervent Chassidic dance, full of devotional ecstasy. The* MERCHANT *now dances with abandon, moving every limb, and takes his course over the green path to the holy ark. Reaching the altar he becomes rigid, transfixed, and slowly walks up the steps. The organ ceases to play. For a moment the* MERCHANT *remains motionless, then he faces slowly about, austere and rigid, turning his head from left to right and from right to left, as if he were considering the crowd upon the benches; he moves his lips as if delivering a speech. Enter the* ORGANIST. *The* MERCHANT *turns to him*). It gets better with each rehearsal. If I only had more time I'd work it out still better. But what's the difference? The first time they'll laugh, anyway, no matter how well I do it. Later, they'll all dance with me. I said, "To-day." Then, to-day it shall be. To-day I reveal myself; to-day I declare myself. Go now to the organ and hold yourself in readiness. Your music certainly will be a success. I only wish that my dance will meet with the same favor. Go now and send the butler in to me.

ORGANIST (*bowing*). The best of luck to you. (*Exit through the door at the right.*)

MERCHANT (*again assumes his serious, stiff attitude and begins to move his lips*).

THE BUTLER (*enters from the door at the right*).

MERCHANT (*descends from the altar*). We are to begin at once. I am going to dress. Let the guests enter. (*Exit through the right hand door.*)

BUTLER (*opens the left hand door and announces*). You are invited to enter. (*There enter at first sev-*

eral USHERS, *followed by the* GUESTS. *All are dressed in fine array, at their head the* WOOL MERCHANT'S WIFE, HIS MOTHER, HIS SON *and* DAUGHTER. *After all the guests have come in the* BUTLER *closes the door, crossing to the right door and standing guard over it. The* USHERS *show the* GUESTS *to their seats and take their places upon either side, forward. The* WIFE, *the* MOTHER, *the* SON *and the* DAUGHTER *are seated at the left, in the front row. All gaze around in bewilderment.*)

VOICES. A synagogue! — A temple! — A holy ark! — An organ! — And everything covered with wool!

A GUEST (*behind the* WOOL MERCHANT'S WIFE). What can all this mean?

WIFE. I'm just as astonished as you are.

GUEST. Didn't you know, either?

WIFE. I'm ashamed to tell. He never permitted me to enter this place and never said a word about what he was building here. And I had to give him my word that I'd never peek into this hall, even if I died from curiosity. But he had to pay me handsomely for the promise.

DAUGHTER. And he paid me handsomely, too.

SON. I got my share, also. "If you don't give me so much and so much, then I'll ferret out your secret." I'm sorry that he is to make it public. It was such an excellent business.

MOTHER. This is a most pleasant surprise to me. To think that he's built a synagogue of his own in his very house — holy ark, sacred scrolls and all. And here was I, thinking what a pity it had been to spend so much effort, from his earliest days, to make a pious Jew of him.

GUEST. But look, an organ; a reformed synagogue.

MOTHER. That makes no difference. Now I know that there will be a son to pray for my soul.

SON. Only let him not ask me to go to the synagogue.

MOTHER. Will it be such a long journey? The synagogue has come to you.

DAUGHTER. Now, mother, you may expect us to have kosher meals once again.

GUEST. Where is he now?

WIFE. I don't know any better than you. He must be behind the door where the butler is standing guard. He is surely not through yet with his dressing.

SON. He'll enter in a prayer shawl, most likely.

MOTHER. That's right! Ridicule your father!

WIFE (*arises, and is about to approach the* BUTLER).

AN USHER (*bars her way*). Kindly be seated. No moving about.

WIFE. But I am —

USHER. I know. Nevertheless, you will be so kind as to remain seated.

WIFE. Where is your master?

USHER. I do not know.

WIFE. Is he soon coming in?

USHER. I do not know. (*He forces her back to her seat.*)

WIFE (*angrily*). "Do not know! Do not know!" (*Takes her seat.*) Very soon we'll all know. So you may as well tell us now!

USHER. Do not know.

SON. I'll take you by the collar and give you such a shaking out. . . .

(*Suddenly the organ commences to play. The door at the right is thrown wide open; first enter two men garbed from head to foot in red wool — in woollen surplices, girdles, shoes and caps — with electric torches in their hands; behind them, four men in purple red wool, bearing upon a board similarly covered, a holy scroll with white woollen cover; behind, two other men in red wool, with electric torches in their hands. At last, the* WOOL MERCHANT *himself comes in, dressed in white wool and wearing a white girdle that sparkles with diamonds. The procession crosses the green path to the holy ark. The organ plays a medley of synagogue, church and Chassidic music. The* MERCHANT *at first moves with slow dance gestures and soon gives himself up to the dance of devotional ecstasy. The audience is astounded, looking on with mouths agape and with a suppressed "Oh!" Now they look at one another with signs of stupefaction and soon must struggle to restrain their laughter. Here and there may be heard the explosion of ill-contained merriment. The men bearing the holy scroll mount the steps of the altar and re-*

main standing in the centre; two of the torch bearers stand at either side of the stage. The MERCHANT *now assumes his stiff posture and advances slowly up the steps. The organ stops playing; the* MERCHANT *faces the audience with an austere, rigid mien; many of the guests are holding their palms across their mouths; the* WIFE, *the* MOTHER, *the* DAUGHTER *and the* SON *sit in dumfounded perplexity.*)

MERCHANT. Ladies and gentlemen: I have assembled you to behold a new service which I myself have established to worship the God that made me — who made me what I now am.

SON (*in a whisper*). Comedy!

MERCHANT (*closes his eyes, as if from the pain of the insult, and then opens them, assuming a stern countenance*). Who has made me what I now am? Answer: Who has made me what I now am?

WIFE. Who, then, *should* have made you what you now are?

MERCHANT. Is that an answer?

SON. You alone made yourself what you are today. You're a self-made man.

MERCHANT. I never expected *you* to be able to recognize true divinity.

MOTHER. God. God has made you what you are to-day.

MERCHANT (*sarcastically*). God! Which God? I'm now fifty years old. Where was that God of whom you prate and whom you always have in mind, where was he up to ten years ago? How much did I not suffer up to ten years ago? What didn't I endure? I was born in poverty, of parents who insisted upon making a rabbi of me.

MOTHER. Would to God you had really become one.

MERCHANT. But I didn't. I wandered from one religious academy to the other, ate at strangers' tables and worked myself up to be a teacher of Hebrew. Then I left home and came to America, worked in a shop as a "greenhorn," became a contractor in boys' trousers, then changed over to petticoats and at last began to deal in wool. Then who made me what I am to-day? (*Silence.*)

DAUGHTER (*diffidently*). The wool?

MERCHANT (*thunders forth, in exaltation*). The wool! (*Stands motionless, his eyes glassy; soon closes them and lowers his head as if in prayer. Then he opens his eyes and views his audience with high-spirited contentment; he speaks in soft toned ecstasy.*) The wool! The wool — God! (*A gasp of horror rises from his hearers. The* WIFE, *the* MOTHER, *the* DAUGHTER *and a few other women bring their hands to their faces. The men look at each other.*) Why do you all sit there so frightened? You imagine that I'm wandering in my speech. You haven't yet understood me. I knew that you would not understand me. I'll explain myself. Know, then, that everything has its own god. The people whom we call primitive and wild knew this. They were nearer to nature and, therefore, knew it. The gods revealed themselves to these primitive folk. Jewish mysticism, too, had a glimpse of this. But it was too greatly influenced by the belief in a single Jewish God, hence did not attain to the real truth.

MOTHER. Woe is me. What words are these?

MERCHANT. I was brought up to believe that everything has its protector in heaven. The truth is, however, that everything has its own god. I have served many a god in my time and none of them desired or was able to help me. Not the god of religious study and not the god of teaching; neither the god of boys' trousers nor the god of petticoats. But when I turned to the wool god, he helped me at once. In ten years he made me a multi-millionaire. (*Raising his voice and with a remarkable expression in his eyes.*) He took me under his protection. He carried me as on wings, higher and higher, higher and ever higher —

VOICES (*frightened*). Oh! Woe, woe! Oh!

MERCHANT (*as if wakened from a trance*). Why your cries of "woe, woe"? You still fail to grasp the truth of my words. But I saw the truth long ago. I recognized my true, my only god, who has carried me to my present heights. And I have reared a temple to him in my house and will worship him to the best of my understanding. And all of you, who have been helped by him through me and been raised aloft, will worship him as I do, together with me, if you do not wish to be forsaken by him and me. (*The organ commences to play anew. The* MERCHANT *turns piously toward the holy ark. Intense unrest prevails in the crowd and the* MERCHANT'S WIFE *wrings her hands. The* MERCHANT *places him-*

self between the holy ark and the board that bears the holy scroll; the board has during this time been lowered from the shoulders of the bearers to their girdles; he turns now to the audience and opens the sacred scroll.) Here is the symbol of my god, the embodiment of his divinity. (*Replaces the scroll upon the board, removes the cover of the scroll, also the inner wrapping and unrolls the scroll. He holds it aloft, spread out, each handle above his head. The scroll turns out to be a white roll of wool.*) This, this is the god that elevated me to my present state. This is the god that from now on you will have to worship together with me! Through him are we all what we are to-day! He has made us rich. He has made us strong. He the good god, the sweet god, the loving god! Him shall we love; him shall we kiss; him shall we embrace; him shall we worship with pious dance. (*He works himself into an increasing ecstatic frenzy, drowning with his cries the mightiest fortissimo of the organ, and at last he breaks into singing at the top of his voice, executing at the same time various dance gestures.*) There is no god like our god! There is no lord like our lord! . . . (*The terror and unrest of the audience now reach their highest pitch; here and there cries are heard, until at last the shouting becomes general. "He is mad! He has gone insane!" The* DAUGHTER *becomes hysterical; the* WIFE *wails, wringing her hands in despair; the* MOTHER *tears her hair; all have left their places and gathered into a group of frightened, shouting, gesticulating persons; above all the din resound the high-*

est notes of the organ; only the men upon the altar, the USHERS *and the* BUTLER *remain calmly in their places during the commotion.)*

SON (*says something to one of the* GUESTS; *the latter dashes out. The* SON *then turns to his mother, sister and grandmother, soothing them with a caressing hand; he is pale and upset, and does not remove his glance from his father*).

MERCHANT (*looks about once again as if wakened from a trance, and cries out*). Silence! (*The organ and the crowd become suddenly still, thus bringing out in greater relief the hysterical weeping of the* DAUGHTER, *the wailing of the* WIFE *and the* MOTHER'S *despairing groans. The* MERCHANT *lowers the scroll of wool slowly to the board and cries again.*) Silence! What sort of words are these? How did you dare to speak thus? Why this sudden outburst of shouting? Why this weeping? Why this tearing of hair? Why this wringing of hands? Why this fright? Does a madman speak as I have spoken to you? I merely wanted to open your eyes. Why do you refuse to understand that I have discovered a truth that you, too, must grasp? Have I not expressed myself clearly? Is anything lacking in my logic? Have I been speaking meaningless words, without any coherence at all? Do the preachers and revivalists speak more clearly than I? Have they any better proofs than I? Think the matter over well, try to understand me, but don't say that I'm insane. Don't be like all the others, who call him crazy whom they do not understand. Or is it better for you that you should call me mad? I do not believe that such a course is to your best interest. Our business still has great need of me. I am still the chosen one of our god. Therefore, it is better for you all to do as I say. Be seated and hear what I have to say further. (*The* GUESTS, *with the help of the* USHERS, *find their seats again, but they are still perturbed, their fright showing in their eyes. The* WIFE, *the* DAUGHTER *and the* MOTHER *can scarcely restrain themselves. The* SON *looks impatiently at the left-hand door.*) Behold. This is the symbol of our god! White wool upon gilded handles. It will remain here in the holy ark, garbed in its cloak. At our services we must all be dressed in wool. Just like me and the gentlemen here. I — in white, because I count myself the High Priest. We shall have other colors, however, besides white and red. We shall institute various degrees, and every degree will have its distinguishing color. We shall pray without words; with dance alone. We shall have only a few hymns. With song and dance we shall remove our wool-god from the holy ark; with song and dance we will carry him about. . . . Don't look at me like that. The world has become godless because we have lost the right road to the gods. I have found my god and the right road to him. Who will follow me upon the true path? Who will be a convert to the truth that I have discovered? Who will serve with me our true lord? Who? Who? Who? See, the wool-god has made us rich! He has made our day bright, he has raised us from the mire and has set us among the most exalted! He has filled us with joy and fortune. He has . . .

THE DOCTOR (*enters, accompanied by the* GUEST *that was dispatched after him*).

MERCHANT (*suddenly breaks off speaking; his eyes distend and his mouth opens wide. All at once he exclaims, wildly*). Who sent for the doctor? Who called the doctor? Out! Out! Everybody! (*To the* USHERS.) Drive them all out! (*The* GUESTS *spring up from their seats and make a dash for the door to the left. The* BUTLER *and the* USHER *thrust them out and close the door.*) Out! You godless wretches! You infidels! You traitors! You ingrates! Out! Out! Out! (*Runs down from the altar with loud outcry.*) Out! out! (*Attacks the* BUTLER *and the* USHER, *who escape through the right-hand door. Then he makes for the men who are standing upon the altar platform. The bearers of the scroll drop the board, and the eight men take to flight through the right door. The* MERCHANT *turns about like a wheel, waving his hands and kicking about.*) Out! Out! (*With the wild growling of a dog he bites his own hands, tears his surplice, scatters the benches in disorder. Soon he becomes weary and exhausted, breathing heavily. He looks around, approaches the altar and sinks to his knees before the wool-god.*) Dear god! Good god! Sweet god!

DOCTOR (*accompanied by several servants, steals cautiously into the room*).

CURTAIN

A DOLLAR

A Comedy

PERSONS

The Characters are given in the order of their appearance.

THE COMEDIAN
THE VILLAIN
THE TRAGEDIAN
ACTOR *who plays* "OLD MAN" *rôle*
THE HEROINE
THE INGENUE
ACTRESS *who plays* "OLD WOMAN" *rôle*
THE STRANGER

A DOLLAR

A cross-roads at the edge of a forest. One road extends from left to right; the other crosses the first diagonally, disappearing into the forest. The roadside is bordered with grass. On the right, at the crossing, stands a signpost, to which are nailed two boards giving directions and distances.

The afternoon of a summer day. A troupe of stranded strolling players enters from the left. They are ragged and weary. THE COMEDIAN *walks first, holding a valise in each hand, followed by the* VILLAIN *carrying over his arms two huge bundles wrapped in bed sheets. Immediately behind these the* TRAGEDIAN *and the* "OLD MAN" *carrying together a large heavy trunk.*

COMEDIAN (*stepping toward the signpost, reading the directions on the boards, and explaining to the approaching fellow actors*). That way (*pointing to right and swinging the valise — to indicate the direction*) is thirty miles. This way (*pointing to left*) is forty-five — and that way it is thirty-six. Now choose for yourself the town that you'll never reach today. The nearest way for us is back to where we came from, whence we were escorted with the most splendid catcalls that ever crowned our histrionic successes.

VILLAIN (*exhausted*). Who will lend me a hand to wipe off my perspiration? It has a nasty way of streaming into my mouth.

COMEDIAN. Stand on your head, then, and let your perspiration water a more fruitful soil.

VILLAIN. Oh! (*He drops his arms, the bundles fall down. He then sinks down onto one of them and wipes off the perspiration, moving his hand wearily over his face. The* TRAGEDIAN *and the* "OLD MAN" *approach the post and read the signs.*)

TRAGEDIAN (*in a deep dramatic voice*). It's hopeless! It's hopeless! (*He lets go his end of the trunk.*)

"OLD MAN" (*lets go his end of the trunk*). Mm. Another stop.

(TRAGEDIAN *sits himself down on the trunk in a tragico-heroic pose, knees wide apart, right elbow on right knee, left hand on left leg, head slightly bent toward the right.* COMEDIAN *puts down the valises and rolls a cigarette. The* "OLD MAN" *also sits down upon the trunk, head sunk upon his breast.*)

VILLAIN. Thirty miles to the nearest town! Thirty miles!

COMEDIAN. It's an outrage how far people move their towns away from us.

VILLAIN. We won't strike a town until the day after tomorrow.

COMEDIAN. Hurrah! That's luck for you! There's yet a day-after-tomorrow for us.

VILLAIN. And the old women are still far behind us. Crawling!

"OLD MAN." They want the vote and they can't even walk.

COMEDIAN. We won't give them votes, that's settled. Down with votes for women!

VILLAIN. It seems the Devil himself can't take you! Neither your tongue nor your feet ever get tired. You get on my nerves. Sit down and shut up for a moment.

COMEDIAN. *Me?* Ha — ha! I'm going back there to the lady of my heart. I'll meet her and fetch her hither in my arms. (*He spits on his hands, turns up his sleeves, and strides rapidly off towards the left.*)

VILLAIN. Clown!

"OLD MAN." How can he laugh and play his pranks even now? We haven't a cent to our souls, our supply of food is running low and our shoes are dilapidated.

TRAGEDIAN (*with an outburst*). Stop it! No reckoning! The number of our sins is great and the tale of our misfortunes is even greater. Holy Father! Our flasks are empty; I'd give what is left of our soles (*displaying his ragged shoes*) for just a smell of whiskey. (*From the left is heard the laughter of a woman. Enter the* COMEDIAN *carrying in his arms the* HEROINE, *who has her hands around his neck and holds a satchel in both hands behind his back.*)

COMEDIAN (*letting his burden down upon the grass*). Sit down, my love, and rest up. We go no further today. Your feet, your tender little feet must ache you. How unhappy that makes me! At the first opportunity I shall buy you an automobile.

HEROINE. And in the meantime you may carry me oftener.

COMEDIAN. The beast of burden hears and obeys. (*Enter the* INGENUE *and the* "OLD WOMAN" *each carrying a small satchel.*)

INGENUE (*weary and pouting*). Ah! No one carried *me.* (*She sits on the grass to the right of the* HEROINE.)

VILLAIN. We have only one ass with us.

COMEDIAN (*stretches himself out at the feet of the* HEROINE *and emits the bray of a donkey.* "OLD WOMAN" *sits down on the grass to the left of the* HEROINE.)

"OLD WOMAN." And are we to pass the night here?

"OLD MAN." No, we shall stop at "Hotel Neverwas."

COMEDIAN. Don't you like our night's lodgings? (*Turning over toward the* "OLD WOMAN".) See, the bed is broad and wide, and certainly without vermin. Just feel the high grass. Such a soft bed you never slept in. And you shall have a cover embroidered with the moon and stars, a cover such as no royal bride ever possessed.

"OLD WOMAN." You're laughing, and I feel like crying.

COMEDIAN. Crying? You should be ashamed of the sun which favors you with its setting splendor. Look, and be inspired!

VILLAIN. Yes, look and expire.

COMEDIAN. Look, and shout with ecstasy!

"OLD MAN." Look, and burst!

INGENUE (*starts sobbing.* TRAGEDIAN *laughs heavily*).

COMEDIAN (*turning over to the* INGENUE). What. You are crying? Aren't you ashamed of yourself?

INGENUE. I'm sad.

"OLD WOMAN" (*sniffling*). I can't stand it any longer.

HEROINE. Stop it! Or I'll start bawling, too. (COMEDIAN *springs to his knees and looks quickly from one woman to the other.*)

VILLAIN. Ha — ha! Cheer them up, Clown!

COMEDIAN (*jumps up abruptly without the aid of his hands*). Ladies and Gentlemen, I have it! (*In a measured and singing voice.*) Ladies and Gentlemen, I have it!

HEROINE. What have you?

COMEDIAN. Cheerfulness.

VILLAIN. Go bury yourself, Clown.

TRAGEDIAN (*as before*). Ho-Ho-Ho.

"OLD MAN." P-o-o-h! (*The women weep all the louder.*)

COMEDIAN. I have —— a bottle of whiskey! (*General commotion. The women stop crying and look up to the* COMEDIAN *in amazement; the* TRAGEDIAN *straightens himself out and casts a surprised look at the* COMEDIAN; *the* "OLD MAN", *rubbing his hands, jumps to his feet; the* VILLAIN *looks suspiciously at the* COMEDIAN.)

TRAGEDIAN. A bottle of whiskey?

"OLD MAN." He — He — He — A bottle of whiskey.

VILLAIN. Hum — whiskey.

COMEDIAN. You bet! A bottle of whiskey, hidden and preserved for such moments as this, a moment of masculine depression and feminine tears. (*Taking the flask from his hip pocket. The expression on the faces of all changes from hope to disappointment.*)

VILLAIN. You call that a bottle. I call it a flask.

TRAGEDIAN (*explosively*). A thimble!

"OLD MAN." A dropper!

"OLD WOMAN." For seven of us! Oh!

COMEDIAN (*letting the flask sparkle in the sun*). But it's whiskey, my children. (*Opening the flask and smelling it.*) U-u-u-m! That's whiskey for you. The saloonkeeper from whom I hooked it will become a teetotaler from sheer despair. (TRAGEDIAN *rising heavily and slowly proceeding towards the flask.* VILLAIN *still skeptical and rising as if unwilling. The* "OLD MAN" *chuckling and rubbing his hands. The* "OLD WOMAN" *getting up indifferently and moving apathetically toward the flask. The* HEROINE *and* INGENUE *hold each other by the hand and take ballet steps in waltz time. All approach the* COMEDIAN *with necks eagerly stretched out and smell the flask, which the* COMEDIAN *holds firmly in both hands.*)

TRAGEDIAN. Ho-Ho-Ho — Fine!

"OLD MAN." He — He — Small quantity, but excellent quality!

VILLAIN. Seems to be good whiskey.

HEROINE (*dancing and singing*). My Comedian, My Comedian. His head is in the right place. But why didn't you nab a larger bottle?

COMEDIAN. Oh Beloved One, I had to take in consideration both the quality of the whiskey and the size of my pocket.

"OLD WOMAN." If only there's enough of it to go round.

INGENUE. Oh, I'm feeling sad again.

COMEDIAN. Cheer up, there will be enough for us all. Cheer up. Here, smell it again. (*They smell again and cheerfulness reappears. They join hands and dance and sing, forming a circle, the* COMEDIAN *applauding.*)

COMEDIAN. Good! If you are so cheered after a mere smell of it, what won't you feel like after a drink. Wait, I'll join you. (*He hides the whiskey flask in his pocket.*) I'll show you a new roundel which we will perform in our next presentation of Hamlet, to the great edification of our esteemed audience. (*Kicking the* VILLAIN's *bundles out of the way.*) The place is clear, now for dance and play. Join hands and form a circle, but you, Villain, stay on the outside of it. You are to try to get in and we dance and are not to let you in, without getting out of step. Understand? Now then! (*The circle is formed in the following order,* COMEDIAN, HEROINE, TRAGEDIAN, "OLD WOMAN," "OLD MAN," INGENUE.)

COMEDIAN (*singing*):

To be or not to be, that is the question,
  That is the question, that is the question.
He who would enter in,
  Climb he must over us,
If over he cannot,
  He must get under us.

REFRAIN

Tra-la-la, tra-la-la,
  Over us, under us.
Tra-la-la, tra-la-la,
  Under us, over us.
Now we are jolly, jolly are we.

(*The* COMEDIAN *sings the refrain alone at first and the others repeat it together with him.*)

COMEDIAN.

To be or not to be, that is the question,
  That is the question, that is the question.
In life to win success,
  Elbow your way through,
Jostle the next one,
  Else *you* will be jostled.

REFRAIN

(*Same as before*)

(*On the last word of the refrain they stop as if dumbfounded, and stand transfixed, with eyes directed on one spot inside of the ring. The* Villain *leans over the arms of the* Comedian *and the* Heroine; *gradually the circle draws closer till their heads almost touch. They attempt to free their hands but each holds on to the other and all seven whisper in great astonishment.*)

All. A dollar!

(*The circle opens up again, they look each at the other and shout in wonder.*)

All. A dollar!

(*Once more they close in and the struggle to free their hands grows wilder; the* Villain *tries to climb over and then under the hands into the circle and stretches out his hand toward the dollar, but instinctively he is stopped by the couple he tries to pass between, even when he is not seen but only felt. Again all lean their heads over the dollar, quite lost in the contemplation of it, and whispering, enraptured.*)

All. A dollar!

(*Separating once again they look at each other with exultation and at the same time try to free their hands, once more exclaiming in ecstasy.*)

All. A dollar!

(*Then the struggle to get free grows wilder and wilder. The hand that is perchance freed is quickly grasped again by the one who held it.*)

Ingenue (*in pain*). Oh, my hands, my hands! You'll break them. Let go of my hands!

"Old Woman." If you don't let go of my hands

I'll bite. (*Attempting to bite the hands of the* TRAGEDIAN *and the* " OLD MAN ", *while they try to prevent it.*)

" OLD MAN " (*trying to free his hands from the hold of the* HEROINE *and the* " OLD WOMAN "). Let go of me. (*Pulling at both his hands.*) These women's hands that — seem so frail, just look at them now.

HEROINE (*to* COMEDIAN). But you let go my hands.

COMEDIAN. I think it's you who are holding fast to mine.

HEROINE. Why should I be holding you? If you pick up the dollar, what is yours is mine, you know.

COMEDIAN. Then let go of my hand and I'll pick it up.

HEROINE. No, I'd rather pick it up myself.

COMEDIAN. I expected something like that from you.

HEROINE (*angrily*). Let go of my hands, that's all.

COMEDIAN. Ha-Ha-Ha — It's a huge joke. (*In a tone of command.*) Be quiet. (*They become still.*) We must contemplate the dollar with religious reverence. (*Commotion.*) Keep quiet, I say! — A dollar is spread out before us. A real dollar in the midst of our circle, and everything within us draws us towards it, draws us on irresistibly.— Be quiet! Remember you are before the Ruler, before the Almighty. On your knees before Him and pray. On your knees. (*Sinks down on his knees and drags with him the* HEROINE *and* INGENUE. "OLD MAN" *dropping on his knees and dragging the* "OLD WOMAN" *with him.*)

"OLD MAN." He-He-He.

TRAGEDIAN. Ho-Ho-Ho, Clown!

COMEDIAN (*to* TRAGEDIAN). You are not worthy of the serious mask you wear. You don't appreciate true Divine Majesty. On your knees, or you'll get no whiskey. (TRAGEDIAN *sinks heavily on his knees.*) Oh holy dollar, oh almighty ruler of the universe, before thee we kneel in the dust and send toward thee our most tearful and heartfelt prayers. Our hands are bound, but our hearts strive toward thee and our souls yearn for thee. Oh great king of kings, thou who bringest together those who are separated, and separatest those who are near, thou who —(*The* VILLAIN, *who is standing aside, takes a full jump, clears the* INGENUE *and grasps the dollar. All let go of one another and fall upon him, shouting, screaming, pushing and fighting. Finally the* VILLAIN *manages to free himself, holding the dollar in his right fist. The others follow him with clenched fists, glaring eyes and foaming mouths, wildly shouting.*)

ALL. The dollar! The dollar! The dollar! Return the dollar!

VILLAIN (*retreating*). You can't take it away from me, it's mine. It was lying under my bundle.

ALL. Give up the dollar! Give up the dollar.

VILLAIN (*in great rage*). No, No. (*A moment during which the opposing sides look at each other in hatred. Quietly but with malice.)* Moreover, whom should I give it to? To you — you — you — you?

COMEDIAN. Ha-ha-ha-ha. He is right, the dollar is his. He has it, therefore it is his. Ha-ha-ha-ha, and I wanted to crawl on my knees toward the dollar and pick it up with my teeth. Ha-ha-ha-ha, but he got ahead of me, Ha-ha-ha-ha.

HEROINE (*whispering in rage*). That's because you would not let go of me.

COMEDIAN. Ha-ha-ha-ha.

TRAGEDIAN (*shaking his fist in the face of the* VILLAIN). Heaven and hell, I feel like crushing you! (*He steps aside toward the trunk and sits down in his former pose.* INGENUE, *lying down on the grass, starts to cry.*)

COMEDIAN. Ha-ha-ha. Now we will drink, and the first drink is the Villain's. (*His proposition is accepted in gloom; the* INGENUE, *however, stops crying; the* "OLD MAN" *and the* "OLD WOMAN" *have been standing by the* VILLAIN *looking at the dollar in his hand as if waiting for the proper moment to snatch it from him. Finally the* "OLD WOMAN" *makes a contemptuous gesture and both turn aside from the* VILLAIN. *The latter, left in peace, smooths out the dollar, with a serious expression on his face. The* COMEDIAN *hands him a small glass of whiskey.*)

COMEDIAN. Drink, lucky one. (*The* VILLAIN, *shutting the dollar in his fist, takes the whiskey glass gravely and quickly drinks the contents, returning the glass. He then starts to smooth and caress the dollar again. The* COMEDIAN, *still laughing, passes the whiskey glass from one to the other of the company, who drink sullenly. The whiskey fails to cheer them. After drinking, the* INGENUE *begins to sob again. The* HEROINE *who is served last throws the empty whiskey glass towards the* COMEDIAN.)

COMEDIAN. Good shot. Now I'll drink up all that's left in the bottle. (*He puts the flask to his lips and drinks. The* HEROINE *tries to knock it away from him but he skillfully evades her. The* VILLAIN *continues to smooth and caress the dollar.*)

VILLAIN. Ha-ha-ha . . . (*Singing and dancing.*)

He who would enter in,
Jump he must over us.

Ho-ho-ho. Oh Holy dollar! Oh Almighty Ruler of the World! . . . Oh King of Kings! Ha-ha-ha. . . . Don't you all think if I have the dollar and you have it not that I partake a bit of its majesty? That means that I am now a part of its majesty. That means that I am the Almighty dollar's plenipotentiary and therefore I am the Almighty Ruler himself. On your knees before me! . . . He-he-he. . . .

COMEDIAN (*after throwing away the empty flask lies down on the grass*). Well roared, lion, but you forgot to hide your jackass's ears.

VILLAIN. It is one's consciousness of power. He-he-he. I know and you know that if I have the money, I have the say. Remember, none of you has a cent to his name. The whiskey is gone. (*Picking up the flask and examining it.*)

COMEDIAN. I did my job well. Drank it to the last drop.

VILLAIN. Yes, to the last drop. This evening you shall have bread and sausage. Very small portions too, for tomorrow is another day. (INGENUE *sobbing more frequently*). Not till the day after tomorrow shall we reach town and that doesn't mean that you get anything to eat there either, but I — I — I — he-he-he. Oh holy dollar, almighty dollar. (*Gravely.*) He who does my bidding shall not be without food.

COMEDIAN (*with wide open eyes*). What? Ha-ha-ha. (INGENUE *gets up and throws herself on the* VILLAIN'S *bosom.*)

INGENUE. Oh my dear beloved one.

VILLAIN. Ha-ha, my power already makes itself felt.

HEROINE (*pushing the* INGENUE *away*). Let go of him, you. He sought my love for a long time and now he shall have it.

COMEDIAN. What? You!

HEROINE (*to* COMEDIAN). I hate you, traitor. (*To the* VILLAIN.) I have always loved — genius. You are now the wisest of the wise. I adore you.

VILLAIN (*holding* INGENUE *in one arm*). Come into my other arm. (HEROINE *throwing herself into his arms, kissing and embracing him.*)

COMEDIAN (*half rising on his knees*). Stop, I protest. (*Throwing himself on the grass.*) "O frailty, thy name is woman."

"OLD WOMAN" (*approaching the* VILLAIN *from*

behind and embracing him). Find a little spot on your bosom for me. I play the "Old Woman," but you know I'm not really old.

VILLAIN. Now I have all of power and all of love.

COMEDIAN. Don't call it love. Call it servility.

VILLAIN (*freeing himself from the women*). But now I have something more important to carry out. My vassals — I mean you all — I have decided we will not stay here over night. We will proceed further.

WOMEN. How so?

VILLAIN. We go forward tonight.

COMEDIAN. You have so decided?

VILLAIN. I have so decided, and that in itself should be enough for you; but due to an old habit I shall explain to you why I have so decided.

COMEDIAN. Keep your explanation to yourself and better not disturb my contemplation of the sunset.

VILLAIN. I'll put you down on the blacklist. It will go ill with you for your speeches against me. Now then, *without* an explanation, we will go — and at once. (*Nobody stirs.*) Very well then, I go alone.

WOMEN. No, no.

VILLAIN. What do you mean?

INGENUE. I go with you.

HEROINE. And I.

"OLD WOMAN." And I.

VILLAIN. Your loyalty gratifies me very much.

"OLD MAN" (*who is sitting apathetically upon*

the trunk). What the deuce is urging you to go?

VILLAIN. I wanted to explain it to you, but now no more. I owe you no explanations. I have decided — I wish to go, and that is sufficient.

COMEDIAN. He plays his comedy wonderfully. Would you ever have suspected that there was so much wit in his cabbage head?

WOMEN (*making love to the* VILLAIN). Oh you darling.

TRAGEDIAN (*majestically*). I wouldn't give him even a single glance.

VILLAIN. Still another on the blacklist. I'll tell you this much — I have decided —

COMEDIAN. Ha-ha-ha. How long will you keep this up?

VILLAIN. We start at once, but if I am to pay for your food I will not carry any baggage. You shall divide my bundles among you and of course those who are on the blacklist will get the heaviest share. You heard me. Now move on. I'm going now. We will proceed to the nearest town which is thirty miles away. Now then, I am off.

COMEDIAN. Bon voyage.

VILLAIN. And with me fares His Majesty the Dollar and your meals for tomorrow.

WOMEN. We are coming, we are coming.

"OLD MAN." I'll go along.

TRAGEDIAN (*to the* VILLAIN). You're a scoundrel and a mean fellow.

VILLAIN. I am no fellow of yours. I am master and breadgiver.

TRAGEDIAN. I'll crush you in a moment.

VILLAIN. What? You threaten me! Let's go. (*Turns to right. The women take their satchels and follow him.*)

"OLD MAN" (*to the* TRAGEDIAN). Get up and take the trunk. We will settle the score with him some other time. It is he who has the dollar now.

TRAGEDIAN (*rising and shaking his fist*). I'll get him yet. (*He takes his side of the trunk.*)

VILLAIN (*to* TRAGEDIAN). First put one of my bundles on your back.

TRAGEDIAN (*in rage*). One of your bundles on my back?

VILLAIN. Oh, for all I care you can put it on your head, or between your teeth.

"OLD MAN." We will put the bundle on the trunk.

COMEDIAN (*sitting up*). Look here, are you joking or are you in earnest?

VILLAIN (*contemptuously*). I never joke.

COMEDIAN. Then you are in earnest?

VILLAIN. I'll make no explanations.

COMEDIAN. Do you really think that because you have the dollar —

VILLAIN. The holy dollar, the almighty dollar, the king of kings.

COMEDIAN (*continuing*). That therefore you are the master —

VILLAIN. Bread-giver and provider.

COMEDIAN. And that we must —

VILLAIN. Do what I bid you to.

COMEDIAN. So you are in earnest?

VILLAIN. You just get up, take the baggage and follow me.

COMEDIAN (*rising*). Then, I declare a revolution.

VILLAIN. What? A revolution!

COMEDIAN. A bloody one, if need be.

TRAGEDIAN (*dropping his end of the trunk and advancing with a bellicose attitude toward the* VILLAIN). And I shall be the first to let your blood, you scoundrel.

VILLAIN. If that's the case I have nothing to say to you. Those who wish, come along.

COMEDIAN (*getting in his way*). No, you shall not go until you give up the dollar.

VILLAIN. Ha-ha. It is to laugh!

COMEDIAN. The dollar please, or —

VILLAIN. He-he-he.

COMEDIAN. Then let there be blood. (*Turns up his sleeves.*)

TRAGEDIAN (*taking off his coat*). Ah! Blood, blood!

"OLD MAN" (*dropping his end of the trunk*). I'm not going to keep out of a fight.

WOMEN (*dropping their satchels*). Nor we. Nor we.

VILLAIN (*shouting*). To whom shall I give up the dollar? You — you — you — you?

COMEDIAN. This argument will not work any more. You are to give the dollar up to all of us.

At the first opportunity we'll get change and divide it into equal parts.

WOMEN. Hurrah, Hurrah! Divide it, Divide it.

COMEDIAN (*to* VILLAIN). And I will even be so good as to give you a share.

TRAGEDIAN. I'd rather give him a sound thrashing.

COMEDIAN. It shall be as I say. Give up the dollar.

HEROINE (*throwing herself on the* COMEDIAN'S *breast*). My comedian! My comedian!

INGENUE (*to the* VILLAIN). I'm sick of you. Give up the dollar.

COMEDIAN (*pushing the* HEROINE *aside*). You better step aside or else you may get the punch I aim at the master and breadgiver. (*To the* VILLAIN.) Come up with the dollar!

TRAGEDIAN. Give up the dollar to him, do you hear?

ALL. The dollar, the dollar!

VILLAIN. I'll tear it to pieces.

COMEDIAN. Then we shall tear out what little hair you have left on your head. The dollar, quick! (*They surround the* VILLAIN; *the women pull his hair; the* TRAGEDIAN *grabs him by the collar and shakes him; the* "OLD MAN" *strikes him on his bald pate; the* COMEDIAN *struggles with him and finally grasps the dollar.*

COMEDIAN (*holding up the dollar.*) I have it! (*The women dance and sing.*)

VILLAIN. Bandits! Thieves!

TRAGEDIAN. Silence, or I'll shut your mouth. (*Goes back to the trunk and assumes his heroic pose.*)

COMEDIAN (*putting the dollar into his pocket*). That's what I call a successful and a bloodless revolution, except for a little fright and heart palpitation on the part of the late master and bread giver.— Listen, someone is coming. Perhaps he'll be able to change the dollar and then we can divide it at once.

"OLD MAN." I am puzzled how we can change it into equal parts. (*Starts to calculate with the* INGENUE *and the* "OLD WOMAN.")

HEROINE (*tenderly attentive to the* COMEDIAN). You are angry with me, but I was only playing with him so as to wheedle the dollar out of him.

COMEDIAN. And now you want to trick me out of my share of it.

"OLD MAN." It is impossible to divide it into equal parts. It is absolutely impossible. If it were ninety-eight cents or one-hundred and five cents or —

(The STRANGER *enters from the Right, perceives the company, greets it and continues his way to left.* COMEDIAN *stops him.*)

COMEDIAN. I beg your pardon, sir; perhaps you have change of a dollar in dimes, nickels, and pennies. (*Showing the dollar. The* "OLD MAN" *and women step forward.*)

STRANGER (*getting slightly nervous, starts somewhat, makes a quick movement for his pistol pocket, looks at the* Comedian *and the others and says slowly*). Change of a dollar? (*Moving from the circle to left.*) I believe I have.

Women. Hurrah!

Stranger (*turns so that no one is behind him and pulls his revolver*). Hands up!

Comedian (*in a gentle tone of voice*). My dear sir, we are altogether peaceful folk.

Stranger (*takes the dollar from the* Comedian's *hand and walks backwards to left with the pistol pointed at the group.*) Good night, everybody. (*He disappears, the actors remain dumb with fear, with their hands up, mouths wide-open and staring into space.*)

Comedian (*finally breaks out into thunderous laughter*). Ha-ha-ha-ha-ha-ha.

CURTAIN

CRIPPLES

A Comedy

PERSONS

First Cripple
Second Cripple
The Workingman
The Soldier
The Sexton

Time and Place: *When and where you please.*

CRIPPLES

A city square; the entrance to a large church. It is long before dawn; from the lantern over the door comes a pale light.

FIRST CRIPPLE (*a maimed arm and a disabled foot, is huddled close to the wall, at the right of the church-door*).

SECOND CRIPPLE (*similarly afflicted, issues from the darkness of the square and becomes visible in the light from the lantern. He notices the* FIRST CRIPPLE *seated before the door and is seized with wild rage*). In my place! May flames devour his entrails! . . . I'll smash his head! . . . He's fallen asleep, it seems. . . . I'll soon send you flying into the gutter! . . . (*About to seize the* FIRST CRIPPLE *by a leg*).

FIRST C. (*suddenly thrusting him away with his foot, bursts into laughter*).

SECOND C. (*falls over, but at once jumps to his feet, ready for a fight*).

FIRST C. (*laughing*). Fooled you, didn't I? So you'll pull me away, will you? And who came first, ha? Who has the best place? Whose hand will be the first to greet the worshippers when they begin to come out? Are you looking for stones? Here; I've got some ready. Ha, ha, ha. . . . And I've got a cane, too. . . . A heavy cane; ha, ha, ha. . . .

SECOND C. Leave that place at once! I'll smash your head for you, I tell you! You louse, son of a bedbug! I'll show you how to kick a fellow away! . . . Get out of that place at once!

FIRST C. Really! Indeed! I'll speed away immediately. . . . Ha, ha, ha. . . . No use! The place belongs to me. You'll never get it back. . . . After every night-service, who will occupy the best place before the door? I! At every fair who will occupy the best place before the door? I! Whose hand will be stuck out before all others? Mine! This very hand. And into whose hand will the ringing coins be first to fall, and most of all? Into mine! Into this very hand. Ring, ring! . . . "God bless you." . . . "God lengthen your years." . . . "May God break your back for you on the very first spot." Ha, ha, ha!

SECOND C. (*almost choking with fury*). I. . . . I. . . .

FIRST C. The best place. . . . The very first seat. . . . A private box. . . . A most excellent site! It feels so good to sit here. . . . It feels so good to stand here. . . . Such a rare site. . . .

SECOND C. It's my place, I say! Away! It's been my place for years. . . .

FIRST C. Ha, ha. . . . A golden place. . . .

SECOND C. (*jumps upon the* FIRST CRIPPLE. *They engage in a struggle and roll down the steps to the sidewalk*).

A MAN (*only one hand, dressed in workingman's*

clothes, appears suddenly from out of the darkness). Hey! Hey! What a fight!

SECOND C. (*on top of the* FIRST C., *and beating him with his good hand as if intent upon killing him*). Now we'll see who takes the best place before the door! Now we'll see whose hand will be the first to greet the worshippers! . . .

FIRST C. You. . . . You. . . . Just let me free my hand. . . . Wait. . . . Just let me. . . .

THE WORKINGMAN (*looks about, then hastens up the stairs to the choice site before the church door*).

SECOND C. (*still punching the* FIRST C.). You will. . . . Yes. . . . You will. . . .

FIRST C. (*frees his good arm*). Now I'll. . . . Now. . . . (*Manages to throw the* SECOND C. *over. Both spring to their feet, glare furiously at each other, ready for another assault. At this juncture, however,* THE WORKINGMAN *decides to smoke a cigarette; the sudden light from his match attracts the attention of the cripples. They turn their gaze toward the church door and notice* THE WORKINGMAN *in the coveted position; whereupon they both limp up the steps to the church door.*)

SECOND C. Hey! You there! That isn't your place!

W. Not my place? Whose is it, then?

SECOND C. It's my place!

FIRST C. It's mine!

W. You don't say so!

SECOND C. It's my place, I tell you!

W. Since I'm standing upon it, it's mine.

Second C. You've no right to be standing on it. I was standing on it. I've been standing on it steadily, do you understand? For years and years. It's my place!

First C. It's mine! I sat on it all night long. I guarded it like a dog. I didn't leave it for a moment. All night long. It's my place. Better leave it without making any trouble.

W. So! That's how it stands!

Second C. Better clear out before you get into trouble!

W. Ha, ha! (*Places his hand upon the face of the* Second C. *and thrusts him away.*) Off with you, carrion-face!

Second C. (*falls. As he gets up he looks about for some stones. He is wild with anger*).

First C. (*hunts likewise for missiles*).

W. I've a whole heap of stones right here. Right at my feet. You must have had them ready. Thanks. And I see a nice heavy cane here, too. (*Grasping the cane.*) Not a bad cane at all. A genuine cudgel. Off, you bandits!

Second C. (*retreating*). It's my place! It's my place!

W. Your place is in hell. In the demon's palace on the devil's tail; that's where your place is!

First C. I lay here all night. What do you mean by seizing it from me? May a three-story bellyache seize you! Who are you, anyway? You're no beggar! You're a thief,— that's what you are! A cut-throat! A pickpocket! You've come to pickpocket the churchgoers! I'm going to call a policeman! . . . Thief! Thief! . . .

W. I'll crush that pate of yours and twist your other leg for you! I'll teach you to cry "Thief!" I am a workingman! . . . Do you understand! I've been a workingman all my life. . . . That's what I was! . . . Lost my arm at my work. . . . So it was all up. . . . No more work. . . . So I must beg. . . . You must show respect for me! Understand! Respect! Away from this place! I've more right to it, understand. I've the right to the very first position. Off with you, eyesores! Beggars!

SECOND C. (*gasping wildly, at first at a loss for words, and finally foaming at the mouth, explosively*). Did you . . . did . . . did you ever hear such claims to respect! You botch-toiler, son of a peasant, how dare you approach us? How dare you class yourself in our company? We are born cripples, I'll have you know. Cripples from our mother's womb, God-given cripples, cripples by the grace of God! We were cripples even when we were in the lap of the Lord. . . . We are chosen cripples!

FIRST C. You've been crippled because you were probably drunk at work. . . . Better leave before you have to!

SECOND C. Better leave, we say, before we make you!

A SOLDIER (*entering from the darkness, and issuing commands in the voice of an officer*). Halt! Attention! Right shoulder, forward, march! (*The three wranglers stare at him.*) Away from the place, all three of you! At once, I say! (*Making out a uniform in the scant light, the three are intimidated and withdraw from the place.* THE SOLDIER *now takes possession of the disputed site.*) That's the way. It's a good thing you show me proper deference. I lost an eye in the war,— an ear,— lost three fingers,— was wounded in the shoulder; got a hole in my side and a medal on my breast. Killed thirteen of the enemy. Rescued our flag from them. Got a medal. The general himself pinned it on me, and shook hands with me. But it's a poor soldier you make with only a single eye, so I took to begging. And the place before the door belongs to me. The very first place. If you understand me, then so much the better for you. If not, I would have to show you how the enemy monkeys executed their rabbits' dash before me. Ha, ha, ha! . . . (*Lights a pipe.*)

FIRST C. The devil! It's only another beggar!

SECOND C. I thought it was a policeman! The devil take him!

W. Here, you, Mr. Hero; the place is not yours. I was standing there.

SOLDIER. Would you like to try and recapture it, perhaps?

W. You just bet!

SOLDIER. You boor! You bumpkin! I was a standard-bearer, and an entire company of enemy monkeys, each one stronger than you, was unable to wrest the flag from me! Do you wish to see how well I can wield this cane,— as if it were a trusty sword? (*Issues commands to himself.*) Fix bayonets! Charge! (*Places his cane as if it were a bayonet.*) Retreat, you band of beggars! I'll stick my bayonet through your belly-buttons, and string you up as on a pitchfork, where all the crows and hounds may devour you. Off with you, pack of womb-bred cripples!

W. You can tell that to them! Not to me. I'm just as good as you are, any day. And even better. I lost my hand in toil. I worked all my life long. Worked since childhood. So that you might go about in idleness. You loafer! I was maimed at my work. And the place at the door of the church belongs to me!

SOLDIER. Ha, ha! I'll yield it to you on the instant. . . . Ha, ha, ha. . . . But let me tell you this much: You say that you *worked* for me. Well, do you know what? Then now you can *beg* for me. All three of you can. I'll permit you to. You should be honored with the task: you'll be begging for a hero! . . . Ha, ha, ha. . . . But I wouldn't trust you. You're all a band of thieves. Sticky fingers. Attention! Salute! And be honored by my permission to stand within three feet of me.

W. You good-for-nothing, you! You worthless wretch! You hero in drawers! That place belongs to me, I tell you. I was standing there when the devil brought you here.

FIRST C. And I was standing there before him. I lay there all night long.

SECOND C. And I've been there for years. The place belongs to me!

THE SEXTON (*appearing at the door*). What's the trouble about? Why all this shouting? You are disturbing the worshippers! You are disturbing the service!

SECOND C. (*excited, clutching at* THE SEXTON *and speaking to him in the third person*). It's a good thing that he appears at this moment! Now the matter will be settled. He, he will. . . . Let him say whom he always sees in this place at every fair and on every holiday? Have I not been standing here for years and years? Does he recall, when he was appointed sexton, that I was the first to congratulate him and to wish him long years and good health and many weddings and many burials? Does he recall? For years and years. . . .

FIRST C. (*seizing* THE SEXTON'S *coat and talking close to his face*). But whom did he see in this place to-night at nightfall, before the first worshipper appeared? Whom did he see huddled together here like a dog? But like a dog they drove me away.

W. Mr. Sexton, I was a toiler, and worked hard all my life. I lost my arm at work. It was caught in the machinery and severed. I was sober, just as truly as you see me now. I didn't take a drop that day. But I was tired, weary with hard toil. My hands could barely move. And my left arm,— ay, ay!— Caught in the wheels. . . . Torn to shreds. Had to have it amputated. And now I must beg.— I've a wife and children. Isn't the best place near the door mine, by right? I was already standing there, when along came —

Soldier (*raising his hand to his hat*). A soldier of the fourth company of the eighteenth regiment.— Killed thirteen of the enemy rats; saved our flag. I bear eight wounds and a medal. Then doesn't the beggar's spot belong to me? Why, they themselves yielded it to me.

First C., Second C., W. That's a lie! That's a lie!

Soldier. I simply issued the order —

The Sexton. Hush-sh-sh! . . . Don't shout!— Let me first know why you should all be disputing for that particular spot, when it makes no difference where you stand?

First C. What do you mean! It's really the best place! It is. . . . It is. . . . (*In a pious manner.*) It is close to the churchdoor, so that it's easier to hear God's word, and a fellow can catch a prayer or two. . . .

Second C. He's lying. He's a hypocrite. That place brings in twice, thrice the amount any other place does, and I don't know how much more.

W. Mr. Sexton, can't you see that the place must go to me?

Soldier. Your grace, the place belongs to a medal and the man that wears the medal.

Sexton. Wait a moment, now. . . . Wait. . . . I wasn't at all aware that a gold-mine was situated right at the church-door.

Second C. And I discovered it.

FIRST C. And I like to hold my ear close to the door. I lay there all night long.

W. Mr. Sexton, one who has toiled as hard as I, deserves a reward.

SOLDIER. Your Highness, the hero is the right man in the right place.

THE SEXTON. None of you will get it.

THE DISPUTANTS. How? — What? — Ha? —

THE SEXTON. That is to say, none of you will get it for nothing. From this day forward the place will be rented.

THE DISPUTANTS (*thunderstruck*). Rented!

SEXTON. Yes. Whoever offers the highest bid will be given the place. How will you rent it: by the year, or per day? I believe that by the year is best. That'll mean less dealing with you. How much am I offered per year? — Quick, now! Quick! — How much? . . .

CURTAIN

THE INVENTOR AND THE KING'S DAUGHTER

PERSONS

THE INVENTOR.
THE KING.
HIS DAUGHTER.
THE PRINCE, HER BETROTHED.
THE COURT JESTER.
THE CHANCELLOR.
TREASURER.
A SERVANT.
A LAME COURTIER.
A BLIND COURTIER.
A FATHER OF DEAF AND DUMB CHILDREN.
A LOVELORN SUITOR.
AN OLD MAN.
AN OLD LADY.
COURTIERS, DAMES, SERVANTS.

THE INVENTOR AND THE KING'S DAUGHTER

"*Once upon a time there was . . .*"

In the large hall of the palace the King *is celebrating the betrothal of his daughter to the* Prince. *Around long tables, placed in the shape of a square with the front side removed, sit the guests — ladies and gentlemen — eating and drinking in unrestrained mirth and with loud laughter, particularly at the antics of the* Jester. *At the head of the centre table sits the* King; *at his right and left, respectively, his daughter and the* Prince; *next to the* Princess *sits the* Chancellor; *next to the* Prince, *the* Treasurer. *In the middle of the open space between the tables, upon a small chair facing a diminutive table, lolls the* Jester, *a very ugly, hunch-backed creature. From various directions morsels of food are thrown to him; wine, too, is poured to him from afar, and he catches it skilfully in his mouth as it flies through the air.*

The Jester. Lo, man can do what is denied a dog. A dog may catch merely a morsel, yet I can catch even drink. And I am but a fool. What canine tricks could not a king be taught! (*The guests dare not laugh, and make sober grimaces.*)

The King. For that jest you get fifty with the lash.

Jester. I simply wished to prove to you how much higher is the least intelligent of mortals than the cleverest of dogs. For man can bite even without teeth.

King. If your teeth are superfluous, I'll have them pulled out for you.

Jester. And it were well if you did so. For if you have them extracted, you do me a great favor. They are so ugly, that often I wish my hump were over my mouth. But you will not do it. Of what use is your jester to you with one ugly feature less?

King. Eat, and close your mouth!

Jester. Silence is the virtue of the wise. Wherefore I must speak, that I may be held a fool. And you must keep silent, that you may be held a sage. Woe to me if I kept silent. Woe to you if you spoke overmuch.

King (*throwing a bone to him*). Catch this, and may you choke.

Jester. Behold! The King is left without a sceptre. The fool wields it now, and now the fool is king.

King. You're drunk, you dog! You're talking too much, and spoiling our festivities. Throw him under the table and see that he utters not a word.

Two Servants (*fall upon the* Jester *and throw him under a table*).

Jester (*barks like a dog*).

King. Silence, there!

JESTER. I am ordered to utter not a word. Wherefore I express myself wordlessly.

KING (*to* SERVANTS). Gag his mouth!

SERVANTS (*bend over the fool and gag him*).

KING. Now we shall have peace, and others may be able to speak.

JESTER (*through his gag*). You would not gain by it!

KING. The fool has made us forget our wine. We drank it, but without giving heed. The splendid wine — it must feel the affront. My friends, I invite you to drink — and with attention. Wine asks to be poured and enjoyed. Its taste goes between our tongues and our palates like the enchanting melody of a violin; but once it arrives at its destination, it spreads through our beings like a glorious orchestra. Drink, my guests, and go beyond your measure. The King has but one daughter — but one betrothal to celebrate. And know this, if you know it not already: the King is happy in the son that his daughter brings to him. My son-in-law — our prince — we may well be proud of him. That my wise daughter should fall so deeply in love with him is greater testimony of his worth than a thousand volumes. You see how red our daughter has become. Ha, ha, ha!

PRINCESS. I feel very warm. May I go to an open window?

KING. Betake your virgin modesty to the window, and let it be kissed and caressed by cool zephyrs.

PRINCE. May I accompany her?

KING. Are you jealous of the breeze? Would you take over the work of the wind? You make her blush all the harder. Go, my prince. With you at her side, the outside world will look in more joyously at her.

PRINCESS AND PRINCE (*bow themselves away and go to the front window, just beyond the end of the table*).

KING (*following them with his glance*). Ha, ha! To the loneliest window, of course. To be alone amidst all the noise and the crowd, and to hear only themselves. My dear chancellor, and you, my dear minister, come closer to me, and let's discuss a certain matter. My guests, let us not disturb you. Permit their Highnesses their solitude in the midst of many, and forget they are here amongst us.

JESTER (*barks from his place under the table, and cries through his gag*). But I would wish that *my* solitude were *not* forgotten!

THE GUESTS (*busy themselves with eating and drinking. The* CHANCELLOR *and the* TREASURER *take seats closer to the* KING).

PRINCESS (*at the window, to the* PRINCE). You read my mind as if my book of thoughts lay open before you.

PRINCE. Your thoughts are mine; mine, too, are your desires. I live only because I carry you so deeply in my heart. The King believes that he does well for us in keeping the guests so long. But we two yearn only for solitude.

PRINCESS. He is so happy.

PRINCE. Yes. I feel nothing against him. It was very kind of him to allow us to leave our places and come here.

PRINCESS (*nestling close to him*). My dear beloved!

PRINCE. I have already forgotten the guests and the excitement. Only your touch intoxicates me, and your words of love resound within me, as if the great hall were filled with wondrous song.

PRINCESS. Shall I tell you how much I love you?

PRINCE. You ask? Never shall I weary hearing you tell it.

PRINCESS. Give me your hand.

PRINCE. Oh, what happiness!

PRINCESS (*presses his hand to her heart*). Do you hear that speech? What am I saying to you?

PRINCE. I could shout for joy.

PRINCESS. From the tips of my toes — I have very pretty toes, and they must be pinker now than ever — to the roots of my red hair — isn't it redder now than before? — a river of love glows through me and inundates me entirely.

PRINCE. Just like the river of love that courses through me. And when the rivers meet —

PRINCESS. Are not all eyes directed on us?

PRINCE. I do not wish to turn my eyes away from you.

PRINCESS. If we should lean far forward out of the window, into the darkness of the night —

PRINCE. Then our lips will believe we are unseen. (*They gaze upon each other passionately, and lean slowly out of the window, closely clasped.*)

A SERVANT (*enters and bows before the* KING).

KING (*interrupting his conversation with the* CHANCELLOR *and the* TREASURER). What have you to say?

SERVANT. A man has come upon a weighty errand, and says that he must see Your Majesty.

KING. A weighty errand? And what is the weighty matter?

SERVANT. He says that he can tell the King alone.

KING. Then let him come to-morrow, or the day after. Have him seized and held under lock and key, until I have slept the betrothal celebration out of all my bones.

SERVANT. He says that it is of the utmost importance to the King and his realm.

KING. Did you not try to drive him off with your halberds, or has he bribed all of you?

SERVANT. We all felt that the man and what he brought were really important.

KING (*eyeing him sharply*). Good. Then bring him here. And if it turns out that this important matter was important only to him, then you shall share his punishment. Nor will it be less for each of you on that account. Go, fetch him! It is too late for you to change your mind.

SERVANT (*bows and leaves*).

KING (*to* CHANCELLOR *and* TREASURER). Can you guess what this may be?

TREASURER. If your majesty cannot guess it, how can we?

CHANCELLOR. Important to King and realm — those were his words. We should have made inquiry whence he came — from what state, across what borders? We haven't even asked whether he was a subject of the King or of a foreign land?

JESTER. Ask me —

SERVANTS (*move against the* JESTER).

JESTER (*barking*). Bow, wow, wow!

KING. Good, fool. I'll ask you. Tell me, what is this important matter?

JESTER. Let them ungag my mouth and I'll crawl out from under the table.

KING. And then you'll tell me?

JESTER. And you will see that I shall answer correctly.

KING (*to* SERVANTS). Remove the gag from his mouth.

JESTER (*crawling out of his place*). It was important that he should come and that I should have my mouth freed and be released from my place under the table — Bow, wow, wow! (*Scampers off across the hall, amidst the uproarious laughter of the guests.*)

SERVANTS (*give chase to him*).

KING. Let him run. Because he was more clever, let him not be punished.

JESTER (*hops over to the* PRINCESS *and the*

PRINCE, *who are leaning out of the window united in a kiss. Stops short and surveys them with various grimaces*). My mouth was never shut for me in *such* a fashion.— That's what is called a kiss. The name I know; I know the word and the sound, but I am unacquainted with the taste. It must be good, though, if folks can't tear away. (*Raising his voice somewhat.*) And if they can so completely forget themselves. . . . (*Louder.*) And if they haven't even heard me. (*Barks very loud.*) Bow, wow, wow!

PRINCESS AND PRINCE (*separate with a start and rise*).

JESTER (*with profuse bows*). Pardon; don't let me disturb you. You may commence all over again, from the beginning. I merely wished to inquire: When is the kiss sweetest — at the beginning, when lips just touch, or — what a fool I am to ask! Surely in the middle, for if it were sweetest at the beginning, then you would quickly cease and begin at the beginning again. As to the end — only the end of sorrows is sweet.

STRANGER (*enters, accompanied by the* SERVANT. *Since the* KING *is engrossed in conversation with the* CHANCELLOR *and the* TREASURER *the* STRANGER *remains standing at a respectful distance. The hall becomes silent. All eyes are turned toward the newcomer*).

PRINCESS. Who is that man?

JESTER. My liberation.

PRINCE. Can't you speak more clearly to the Princess?

JESTER. It is just as I say. Because he came I was liberated.

KING (*to the* STRANGER). Approach and tell what important matter has brought you to me.

STRANGER (*approaches and bows*).

KING. Who are you?

STRANGER. I am an inventor, a loyal subject of your Majesty, and have contrived a great invention.

KING. And did you have to come to me with it just at this moment, in the midst of my festivities?

INVENTOR. I had to come with it this very moment. Before I was not fully ready with it, and afterward it would have been too late.

KING. What is your invention?

INVENTOR. The greatest that the world has ever known.

KING. That does not make the matter clearer to me.

INVENTOR. If you accept my invention, you will increase your own happiness and that of your subjects forever. Nay, the whole world will turn to you, as to its greatest savior, and you will become the ruler of the earth.

KING. Then how is it that *you* have not become that ruler?

INVENTOR. If you should be that, then I should become it, too. And I need your help.

KING. The matter is still hazy to me.

JESTER. Behold! A second fool has come to light!

KING. What is your invention? And how can I be of help?

INVENTOR. First let me tell you all about myself. My ancestry, and my pedigree.

KING. And what has that to do with your invention? I wish to know that alone.

INVENTOR. My King, first *I* came, then my invention. And moreover, my discovery is so great, that only through the immense power that lay accumulating through generations, finally to be embodied in me, was I able to accomplish it.

KING. And you descended from a long line of sages?

INVENTOR. Quite the opposite, my King. I speak of accumulated power — power of mind, which was not used, not expended, not employed.

KING. Be brief, then. Tell us of your ancestry.

INVENTOR. Neither my father nor my grandfathers and great grandfathers, for seven generations past, on both my maternal and paternal sides, have died a natural death. They all met their end upon the gallows for robbery, crime and murder. (*A roar of laughter.*)

CHANCELLOR (*laughing*). And how about the female ancestors?

JESTER. Take all the maidens away. They must not hear this.

INVENTOR. You are right. My mother and my grandmothers and my great grandmothers, also on both sides, were public houses for friends and guests and passers-by. (*A din of laughter.*)

FIRST COURTIER. And how was it before the seven generations?

SECOND DITTO. How do you know who was your father?

THIRD DITTO. For seven generations and even longer, filth was accumulating. . . .

FOURTH DITTO. Crime and prostitution. . . .

JESTER. Out of seven generations of ugliness I was born — the ugliest of all.

KING. Enough. The gallows has kept him waiting all too long, so this churl comes to remind it of its due.

INVENTOR. You may hang me when you have heard all I have to say. My King, in every fool there is hidden at least a spark of spirit and wisdom; in every vagabond, a drop of honesty. And in the seven criminal generations of my ancestors wisdom and honesty kept the tiny spark aflame. Spark by spark it was treasured up from generation to generation — drop by drop — and all this hoard was delivered to me.

TREASURER. A bedbug could carry all the hoard.

JESTER. And thereupon the sparks drank all the drops; and then the drops extinguished all the sparks. So what was left? (*Laughter.*)

INVENTOR (*proud, firm*). *I* have made the greatest of inventions.

CHANCELLOR. And this greatest invention of

yours is — a mere invention, a manufactured lie. (*Laughter.*)

INVENTOR. I have made the greatest of inventions. (*The laughter ceases.*) It means world-supremacy for the King; it means a blessing to humanity; it means, perhaps, eternal life.

KING. His very words nauseate me to the core.

INVENTOR. Your Majesty, I was overcome with nausea at myself. The crimes of seven generations weighed heavily upon me, and I pondered continually how to redeem them — how to make good what seven generations had made so evil. The filth of seven generations clung to me, and I longed for purity, seeking how to cleanse myself. This it was that led me to the thought that I must accomplish something for which mankind would be forever grateful. And for years I labored and thought severely, seeking without rest, with one goal alone before my eyes. And I prayed long to God — I dwelt in deep solitude, secluded from the whole world, alone with my studies, my thoughts and my God. And God heard my prayers and answered them.

KING (*with disgust*). What is your invention?

INVENTOR. God has permitted me to peer into the secrets of His creation, to behold that which none has beheld before me, to discover powers in nature that none has ever before suspected.

TREASURER. And just as they have never been suspected, neither are they there.

INVENTOR. Do you know the sun?

TREASURER. I know her well, but I have never had the honor of being introduced.

INVENTOR. Of course, you know the sun. All of you know the power that you feel. You know that you need the sun for the growth of your crops. You know, too, how necessary it is to your good humor. Yet the sun is not in your power. It serves you, but you cannot yet command it. At night you have to wait till day arrives. And if the day brings rain, then you must wait until the clouds have emptied and gone by.

CHANCELLOR. Wondrous are the tales he tells to us. And is this the important news that brought you hither?

TREASURER. Soon he will tell us that when the sun shines it is bright, and that when darkness comes it is a sign that the sun is not shining.

INVENTOR. *I* have discovered how to harness the sun's rays to my will, and to place them in my service.

CHANCELLOR. Perhaps this fellow's the Devil! Are you a sorcerer?

INVENTOR. Your Majesty, I desire to be taken seriously.

KING. Do not interrupt him.

INVENTOR. I am no sorcerer, neither have I done anything supernatural. God has helped me to utilize His power. He has aided me in constructing a device which catches the rays of the sun, and through it I can perform all manner of miracles that the sun performs, and even more. For to the power of the sun is added the wisdom of man and his piety.

TREASURER. How ill that sounds from his mouth!

KING. What miracles can you perform?

INVENTOR. I have told you already, my King. Or did you misunderstand me? All the wonders of the sun and more. Through my device night can be made to cease, cold can be banished; you can attach it to your chariot and it will bear you faster than the fastest steeds. You will no longer need oars for your vessels, yet you will cut through the waves of the most distant seas faster than ever. It will raise you aloft, as on the wings of the mightiest eagle; it will bore you a tunnel to all the treasures of earth's depths. The power that is locked within it can heal wounds that have hitherto been beyond cure. . . .

LAME COURTIER. Can it straighten my limbs?

INVENTOR. If you have not lost your feet entirely.

BLIND COURTIER. Can it restore the light of my eyes?

INVENTOR. If your eyes have not utterly leaked out.

ANOTHER COURTIER. Can it make the deaf hear? Can it make the dumb speak? I have two little children, a son and a daughter, as beautiful as cherubs, but both are deaf and dumb.

INVENTOR. Their speech will soon be gladdening your heart.

LOVELORN SUITOR. I am lovesick. The glorious maiden of my desire has locked her heart and bosom against me. Can your device assist me here?

INVENTOR. Should you desire to commit suicide

you will find in my contrivance the speediest, least painful of deaths.

A Lady. Can it restore youth?

Inventor. I assure you you will look like your own daughter's daughter.

Lady. The impudence! I'm still a girl myself!

Second Lady (*bashfully*). Can it give beauty?

Inventor. As beautiful as you would wish yourself.

Jester (*with an outcry*). Can it *really* give beauty?

Inventor. You will not know yourself. Your yellow, decayed teeth will turn white again and sound. Those long tusks that protrude from your mouth will be filed down and take their place in a row with all their smaller neighbors. Your hump will be crushed in between your shoulder-blades and dissolve into muscles and fat and you will gain in stature what your hump robbed you of.

Jester (*excited*). Beware, I tell you! I know sharper gibes than that!

Inventor. I am far from jesting, and only once in all my life have I laughed — the moment when I saw that my invention was a success.

Jester (*with bated breath*). And can you really make me beautiful?

Inventor. You will soon be convinced. You will feel as if newborn.

Jester (*stirred to the highest pitch*). I shall be beautiful! My hump will dissolve and my height will increase! My mouth will be shorn of its terror!

Fair shall I be! Yes, fair! And then am I fool no longer! Have you beheld a fair one spat upon the face? Have you beheld a handsome one chastised with the lash? Have you heard of one that's fair suffering ugly treatment? Oh, I shall be fair — freed of folly — and then I, too, will kiss a pretty maiden. Kiss — a — pretty — maiden! At the window, wide open to night's sheltering darkness, bosom to bosom pressed tight! (*To the* LADIES.) Hey! Who of you will wish to be carried off by me? I long to be abducted by you all! Handsome shall I be, and as to brains, I've always —

KING. He has gone mad. Have him quieted.

JESTER (*hops away*). I shall be handsome! I shall be fair! Bow, wow, wow!

AN OLD COURTIER. And can you really bring back youth?

INVENTOR. I have already answered that question for one of the ladies. I can make you young. And as I have said — my invention will perhaps bring life everlasting.

OLD COURTIER. Why your "perhaps"?

INVENTOR. How can I be certain? Life everlasting alone can prove it. I assert only that of which I am certain.

CHANCELLOR. You said before that it can also kill.

INVENTOR. You find in it what you seek. It has the power to give eternal life, and is at the same time a deadly weapon. In war you will be able, with its aid, to annihilate the King's enemies as if by sunstroke.

TREASURER. Can it also transmute stone and sand into gold?

INVENTOR. How strange! That selfsame claim was on my tongue. You took the very words from out my mouth. Yes; my device most surely has that power.

KING. Have you it with you here?

INVENTOR. No, and yes. No, because it is not here in completed form. Yes, because it is in my brain and ready to be set up at any moment.

KING. When will you set it up for me?

INVENTOR. When your majesty will consent to lend me aid.

KING. And how can I lend you aid?

INVENTOR. My King, the Lord has beheld my yearning for purification and sent me this invention. He was good to me. He heard my prayers. The earth, all earth, will bless my name forever; my name will blaze like a shining star, eternally, upon the firmament of humanity. But, like the nebulous tail of a glorious comet, there will trail after me the shame and disgrace of seven evil generations. All the boons that I will bring through my invention will not suffice to extinguish the spot of my brilliant sun. But I do not wish to carry the spot upon me; it must be wiped out in its entirety. I wish to stand before the world unstained. You can help me.

KING. I have already asked you, How? How would you be cleansed?

INVENTOR. Through union with the highest purity.

KING. And that is?

INVENTOR. Your daughter. (*A stir among the guests.*)

KING. What?

INVENTOR. I want your daughter for my wife.

PRINCESS (*clutching the* PRINCE, *with an outcry*).

PRINCE (*seizes the hilt of his sword*).

INVENTOR. Perhaps in generations yet to come humanity will endow me with another ancestry. Ashamed to own a foul soul as a savior, it will ascribe new parentage to me, of pure, unsullied lineage. But as a King's son-in-law I should at once attain that which otherwise I must await for generations. Your royal splendor would at once illumine my entire pedigree and cause my father and mother to be forgotten.

KING (*breathes with difficulty; eyes the* INVENTOR *with wild fury, clinches his fist, as if seeking a punishment for the man*).

INVENTOR. You are angry, your majesty? Is my request, then, so much too great? Here I have brought all mankind's happiness. Do I not, then, deserve the great purification? I have brought you, my King, power over all and seek to be uplifted through you. Does the exchange seem not worth while to you? O King, the Lord sent the invention to me that I might thus reach you.

KING (*throws his wineglass at the* INVENTOR *and thunders*). Remove him from my sight! Take him away! Hang him! Burn him! No. Torture him as none before him has been tortured! Chancellor, Treasurer, all my counsellors, all you wise and all you wicked guests of mine, get together and think out the most exquisite punishments! (*The* SERVANTS *move slowly and hesitantly toward the* INVENTOR.)

INVENTOR. O King, are you in doubt about my claim? Would I have risked my life and come to you with a device that had not proved itself? Do I not know what my end would be if I deceived you? Do you think that I asked your credence only on my word? Promise me your daughter — only give me your pledge — that she will become my wife when you shall learn that all I claim is just as I have said.

PRINCESS (*in great excitement*). And even if it be true — even if it be a thousand times true, never will I be his wife! And if it perform even more than he claims for it — I love my Prince! I love my Prince!

KING (*to* SERVANTS). Why so slow, you hounds? Do you wish to be those from whom he will learn how great his tortures are to be? Take him away as fast as possible! Give him his reward. (*To the* SERVANT *who announced the* INVENTOR'S *arrival.*) — And you, who smuggled him into the hall, who so earnestly assured us of his importance, unless you care to share his fate with him, as I had promised, execute every torture that will be invented for him. And see that you invent a few more, to make up for what the others have omitted.

INVENTOR (*warding off the servants*). Grant me but a few words more. God's will must be done. Daughter of the King, you were pointed out to me by the Lord. Even as the invention, so from Him, too, comes the thought that I must demand you for my wife. You have been chosen by Him for my great purification. See, I place within your tender hands the happiness of all humanity.

PRINCESS (*presses more closely to the* PRINCE). Oh, let him not address me!

KING. Why is he still permitted to speak?

JESTER (*cries out*). I want to be handsome! I want to be fair!

LAME COURTIER. He can straighten my limbs!

BLIND DITTO. He will restore the light to my eyes!

INVENTOR. The ills of all humanity cry out aloud to thee, beauteous daughter of the King.

PRINCESS. No! No!

KING. Remove that heap of filth, I say!

PRINCE (*springing suddenly across the table, dashes toward the* INVENTOR *and runs him through the breast with the sword*). Here is your purification, you scoundrel, you mangy dog!

INVENTOR (*clutches his wound*). The greatest crime of the ages has been committed! (*Falls dead.*)

JESTER (*with outcry falls over his body. Murmur among the guests*).

KING. Take him away and throw him to the hounds! What are you murmuring about there? Did you wish your King to be a mat upon which a man who rose from the filth of hell should wipe his feet? You are dismissed. The festivities are over. Good night to you all. Come, my daughter!

Smooth your forehead and drive from your memory all thought of this interruption. We'll do better at your wedding. Hell, let us hope, has no more filth to spew. Come, Prince! Let me grasp your hand. If I could jump a table as well as you, I, too, should have drawn my sword. And yet you were a trifle hasty there. You released him all too soon from his well-merited tortures. Chancellor! Minister! Good-night! (KING, PRINCESS, PRINCE, CHANCELLOR, MINISTER *and many other guests file out.*)

SERVANTS (*thrust away the* JESTER *and carry off the* INVENTOR'S *body*).

JESTER (*with a tearful voice*). Ah! . . . Do you know what it is to be ugly? Do you know what it is to carry a hump on your back all your life? Do you know what it is not to know what a kiss from a maiden tastes like? And he had it in his power. . . . Ah! . . .

LAME COURTIER. He would have straightened out my foot.

BLIND DITTO. My sight would have been restored.

FATHER OF DEAF AND DUMB CHILDREN. My dear children! My poor, miserable, deaf and dumb darlings!

LADY. What will the world say when it learns of this?

COURTIER. The world will say: There was one who strove for greater purity. God helped him, but when he came to human beings he was slain.

SECOND DITTO. The world will say: There was

a King who abjured world domination, because he did not wish to unite his family with that of an impure churl.

SECOND LADY. The world will say: There was a Princess who refused immortality because she loved.

AN OLD COURTIER. No, no. The world will curse. He brought to her the gift of eternal sun . . . eternal youth . . . life everlasting. . . .

THIRD LADY. The world will be steeped in sorrow.

CURTAIN

DIPLOMACY

A Satire

PERSONS

THE CHANCELLOR.

HIS WIFE.

THE LEADER OF THE YELLOW PARTY.

THE LEADER OF THE BLACKS.

THE LEADER OF THE BLUES.

THE LEADER OF THE GRAYS.

A SECRETARY.

THE MOB, *composed of adherents of the various parties.*

TIME AND PLACE — *Of a fairy-tale.*

DIPLOMACY

The spacious ante-room of the chancellery. In the background, high, wide windows; benches running along the entire length of the wall. To the right, two doors leading to the CHANCELLOR'S *quarters. The forward door opens into the* CHANCELLOR'S *cabinet, where he is now engaged. To the left, a broad staircase.*

The leader of the YELLOWS *and the leader of the* BLACKS *are engrossed in conversation, at the same time keeping a close watch upon the cabinet door.*

THE LEADER OF THE YELLOWS (*garbed in a fantastic costume of yellow*). Live and let live, that has always been my motto. I demand much for me and mine, but I am willing to let the other fellow have his share; nor do I forget my folk and fatherland. Gladly will I support you in your demands, if they do not conflict with my own, and if I feel that mine are quite secure.

THE LEADER OF THE BLACKS (*garbed in a fantastic costume of black*). My demands have always been the most important, dear friend. You think only of yourself, while I consider all the people.

YELLOW. Ah! I can turn your own words in

my favor and against yourself. I maintain that not until my demands have been granted will our people truly live.

BLACK. But you think merely of the body. I minister to the soul.

YELLOW. Excellent. Then you and I must be one. We must support each other and work hand in hand. Then will the whole people be well provided for — both in body and soul.

BLACK. The soul comes first.

YELLOW. We'll never come to an understanding. You are so frightfully obstinate. You wish to be the sole leader. I tell you frankly and like a friend: you'll never succeed. And in the end, you'll lose to me.

BLACK. What? You dare —

YELLOW. Be calm! We've got a-talking and strayed far from the point. Let's get back to the present moment. For today, at least, we unite in a single demand.

BLACK. From different points of view, naturally.

YELLOW. Oh, yes. Of course. Yet you need the war no less than I. It is precisely as necessary to your interests as to mine. The people have lost their fear of God and the churches are empty —

BLACK. That's the deepest disgrace of all!

YELLOW. War will fill them for you once again. It is your duty to demand the war in the name of God and true piety. It is *our* God that sends us forth to battle. He is with us, if we are with Him —

BLACK. You speak the truth.

YELLOW. And He will stand by us. He will drive the enemy before us, and will visit annihilation upon them — with the help of our army and our weapons. He will deliver into our hands the lands of the foe and make the enemy's children our slaves. And where once we had dangerous competitors we will, with the help of the Lord, have vassals to do our will. I predict that the people will throng to your churches day and night, to pray for the victory of our arms. And your collection plates will become fuller and fuller.

BLACK. My plates! — who talks of plates?

YELLOW. Very well.— Let it be your bowls.— And as soon as the war is over, imagine! You will convert the enemy to our faith. Consider what will be your reward for that!

BLACK. You harp eternally on reward.

YELLOW. I mean both in this world and in the next.

BLACK. The main point is that I desire a free hand in converting the enemy. If it cannot be accomplished with kind, friendly words, then I shall be able to do it with the right and might of the victor.

YELLOW. So then — we're agreed.

BLACK. I am certainly for war. I *must* favor war. It is God's will. But you — why do you demand war with the Turanian?

YELLOW. I believe I have explained that to you

already. I believe, moreover, that *I* am the most important personage in the matter.

Black. You, the most important? You, with your donkeys that he has seized?

Yellow. At any rate the donkeys furnish an excellent reason for declaring war against him. The war that will profit both you and me considerably.

Black. God, God is the most important consideration. And God alone is the reason.

Yellow. Very well. I concede your point. The donkeys are merely the Lord's ambassadors. So then,— give me your hand upon it. We'll appear before the Chancellor united, with a single purpose and a single demand. And thus we shall get our war. You may now prepare your prayers and call down upon us the blessings of Heaven. (*Makes a low bow to the* Black.)

Black (*blesses the* Yellow *with a silent movement of the lips and a pious rolling of the eyes*).

Yellow. And now.— Oh, yes: another thing. We must stand firm. We must dictate to the Chancellor. We must. (*Interrupts himself and looks towards the staircase.*) Here comes the leader of the Blues striding proudly up the stairs. (*Runs over toward the* Blue.) War!

Blue (*garbed in a fantastic costume of blue, with sword and coat of mail*). What? Has the chancellor already reached a decision?

Yellow. No. Not a word as yet from the chancellor. He's been locked in his cabinet for the past twenty-four hours —

BLUE. I know that. Then what was the meaning of your cry of "War!"

YELLOW. It meant that he and I are as much in favor of this war as you.

BLUE. As I? Ha, ha!

YELLOW. What? Aren't you for war?

BLUE. For *war* — yes!

YELLOW. That means. . . . Oh, I see. . . . I see! . . . War is your profession, your business and your bread.

BLUE. Bah! Business, bread, profession! The shopkeeper translates it into his own language and makes a shopkeeper of me! *War* — a business! *War* — a profession! Ha! *War,*— ah, that is something a shopkeeper cannot understand! War is the sublimest vocation, the noblest of arts!

BLACK. Forget not the soldiers of the Lord.

BLUE. The word comes after the sword. How could you ever advance God's word if the sword did not cut a passage for it? Ah, what would mankind have been, if God had not blessed it with war? It would have overrun the earth like mice, and only pestilence would save the world from over-population. War, too, ennobles man, makes him courageous and strong and wakes him to deeds of daring! War —

YELLOW. Enough! What you say is good, and true! The main point is that we are unanimous!

BLUE (*scornfully*). Pah!

YELLOW. We work hand in hand.

BLUE (*in disgust*). He-he!

YELLOW (*irritated, loudly*). We all stand for war. In the name of our people and our country.

BLACK. And the Lord.

YELLOW. And our Lord.— Naturally, self-understood — we must declare war against the God-forsaken Turanian. He seized our donkeys. . . .

BLACK. He denies our faith.

YELLOW. For that he shall pay us dearly.

BLUE (*drawing his sword*). That he will!

BLACK. Oh, Heaven, bless Thou our arms!

BLUE. I've seen to that already. My army is vast and well trained, and itches for combat. It's impossible to hold the soldiers back, to calm them down. Before the heathen has rubbed the sleep out of his eyes, he'll lie like a nut between the divisions of my army — Crack! And crushed he is like a hollow shell! War! War!

YELLOW. And then we'll take back our donkeys with a hundred per cent. interest!

BLACK. And we'll open his heart and his ears so that he may receive God's word and conceive the true mercy of the Lord!

YELLOW. Here comes the leader of the Grays. Shall we waste much time arguing with him? We'll inform him that we've decided upon war. That will suffice him. And if he proves obstinate —

BLACK. It would be better if we come before the chancellor as a united people.

GRAY (*garbed in a fantastic gray costume, approaches with a humble bow*). Good day to you, gentlemen! (*The* YELLOW *and the* BLACK *reply with official bows. The* Blue *turns away and fences with his sword.*)

Gray. What's the news? Has his Excellency yet let himself be heard from?

Yellow. Do you mean whether he is snoring?

Gray (*undecided whether to laugh or not. He commences to laugh and stops at once in embarrassment*). I mean — that is: — How stands it with the war?

Blue (*brandishing his sword as if in battle*). War! War!

Yellow. We stand firm for war.

Black. It is God's will.

Gray. Yes, yes — God's will — Is war sure? — I think — we think —

Blue (*mockingly continues to conjugate the verb*). You think, they think.

Gray (*confused*). He-he — we think that the war is —

Yellow. Very necessary for our land and people.

Black. And our religion.

Gray. Very necessary. . . . He — he. . . . But we think —

Yellow. From whatever standpoint you view the matter, there must be war: from the standpoint of patriotism, religion, humanity, morality, hygiene, commerce and — and so forth. We believe that there is no room for any other opinion here. If you and your constituents think otherwise, then you haven't considered the matter carefully, or judged it aright. You have surely looked at it only from the gray standpoint,— and that standpoint is very narrow and short-sighted and — and gray. You just leave everything to us. We desire and have always desired only the welfare of our people and our entire country. Go back to your party and bring them our decision. Tell them that they may rest assured. The war will prove a blessing to all.

Black. From His Beloved Name.

Blue. War! Ta ra ra! War — Hurrah!

Gray (*scratching his head*). We talked the matter over and discussed it thoroughly. We see that we have nothing to gain from the war —

Blue. Gain! Gain! Must everything be reckoned in weights and measures, and in filthy coin! The honor of our arms is the greatest gain; a well-conducted war is in itself the highest profit.

Black. We will win the conquered Turanian for our faith — that is the greatest gain of all.

Yellow. The Turanian must not grow greater or more powerful. To render him powerless is a huge gain for all of us.

Gray. He — he, yes, but —

The Black, Blue and Yellow (*impatiently*). But! — But! — But! —

Gray (*timidly*). We believe that *we* will lose very much by the war.

Yellow. Not so! You believe what is very silly.

Black. Believe only in God and His mercy.

Yellow. What have you to lose, anyway? You retain your fields.

GRAY. But consider. . . .

YELLOW. We've considered everything thoroughly. We've considered your interests as well as ours. You must raise yourself to a higher standpoint. Your eyes must be able to encompass more distant horizons.

BLACK. You must learn to recognize the will of the Lord.

YELLOW. The war is a necessity, imposed upon us by the Lord Himself, as you have just heard from our representative of God. Ask him to bless you, and —

BLACK (*murmurs a prayer and rolls his eyes piously*).

YELLOW. And return to your party and tell them that they have seen the matter in the wrong light. (*To the others.*) Do you know what? Let's all go down to our people and announce to them that the party leaders are unanimous in their decision for war. Such news will rouse them more than ever for war. Perhaps the popular demonstration will hasten the chancellor in his slow deliberations.

BLACK. That's a splendid suggestion.

GRAY. I'd be very grateful if you'd talk matters over a little with my people.

BLUE. I'm off to drill my men a little.

YELLOW. Let us be off, too! (*Casting a glance towards the* CHANCELLOR's *cabinet.*) Not a sound comes from that room.— Then let the street make itself heard. (*All file out, the* GRAY *at the rear. For a while the room is empty, but soon the* CHAN-

CELLOR'S WIFE *comes hurrying up the stairs, heavily veiled, hastens over to the* CHANCELLOR'S *door and knocks.*)

A SECRETARY (*appearing at the door*). What would you have?

THE CHANCELLOR'S WIFE. I want to see the Chancellor.

SECRETARY. Impossible. (*About to shut the door.*)

WIFE. Tell him that his wife is waiting here for him.

SECRETARY. Oh, pardon me! (*Disappears.*)

WIFE (*raises her veil and looks toward the door in joyous anticipation*).

THE CHANCELLOR (*comes out*). My darling, my precious. You here?

WIFE (*throwing her arms about his neck*). Oh, I could endure it no longer, not to see you for twenty-four hours!

CHANCELLOR. The question is of supreme importance. It cannot be prolonged, and I will settle it quickly, like a true servant of my people.

WIFE. But to abandon me so? Couldn't you tear yourself away for a moment and run across to me? Is this our honeymoon?

CHANCELLOR. My darling, you'll have to forgive me. I am performing my duty. Even now I shall have to send you away at once. Thanks for having come. You brought me a breath of happy relief, and now I shall return to my work with renewed vigor. My precious love —

WIFE. You shall not dismiss me so easily. And if you do, I refuse to obey you, and cling tightly to you! Oh! Not to have seen or heard you for twenty-four hours!

CHANCELLOR. Did I not feel it, too? Did it not oppress me, likewise?

WIFE. No. You forget me entirely. You're absorbed altogether in your faithfulness to the people and the country, and your young wife no longer exists for you.

CHANCELLOR. You mustn't speak like that to me. You yourself don't believe what you say.

WIFE. On the contrary, I believe it firmly. You value your duty more than your love.

CHANCELLOR. You may as well say that my sleep, too, is more to me than my love, for each night I leave you and journey off to far-away, far-away slumberland —

WIFE. Yes, but in my arms,— at my side! And often I watch over you when sleep refuses to come to me. In silence I enjoy the lines of your face, and suddenly I see you smile, and I know that you are smiling to me in your dream, and then I fall asleep so happy! . . . Ah, tonight I did not close my eyes. I tossed from side to side with the most uneasy thoughts.

CHANCELLOR. My poor darling! But let that be. Once my burdensome task is removed from my shoulders, I'll come flying to you as on the wings of an eagle, and what we have lost today, we'll make up for tenfold. Go now, my love —

Wife. No, I will not go. I must sit with you a while. Take me into your cabinet with you.

Chancellor. Absolutely impossible. My secretaries occupy every desk and chair. And moreover, they themselves have not been home for the past twenty-four hours.

Wife. And their wives are not —?

Chancellor. Allowed to come here. And what is not permitted to my secretaries I will not permit to myself.

Wife. But I am already here! Come, sit down with me — there on that bench. I'll sit down beside you, feel your presence, drink in the sight of you — (*Draws him to the bench.*)

Chancellor. Further from the window; they should not see us from the outside. Otherwise they'll besiege me again. (*Steals a glance through the window.*) What a crowd! The whole populace has gathered on the square. It is impatient and will become more so. It's really a crime for me to be sitting here calmly with you.

Wife (*nestling to him*). Come, come. It isn't yet so grave as all that. The little time that I'll steal from the nation's affairs, it may well grant me. And why should the nation be more important than I? Twenty-four hours! — And more: the nation has robbed me of you entirely. You're sitting by me this very moment as if on pins and needles. You neither look upon me nor see me. You hear my words but your thoughts are there with your secretaries.

Chancellor (*arises suddenly and looks again stealthily through the window*). What a seething commotion outside! What burning impatience! The populace has been incensed for war and its war spirit grows with each moment. It knows not why, nor wherefore. "War! War!" it cries, blinded, betrayed by robbers that seek to wax richer and richer. War! War! Say rather Murder and Blunder. How I hate every war,— the most shameful of crimes! They seek through war only to conquer, to fill their coffers, to aggrandize themselves at the expense of the vanquished. That is what the bands of robbers desire who attack the citizens of their towns or the peacefully-travelling caravans in the desert. And if the robbers are criminals, sure of a death-sentence, when caught, why is not the State that goes forth to robbery a criminal? Murder is murder, and shall I be a murderer? Shall I be a tool to serve the end of plunderers?

Wife. Oh, my love, can't you forget all this for a while and belong to me entirely — for a moment, for the smallest moment? (*Nestles closely to him.*)

Chancellor (*as if suddenly awakened, embraces her and looks at her with a penetrating glance.*) To forget for a moment — to belong to you —you! (*Takes her to him in a long, passionate, vehement kiss.*) In that moment I was yours completely. I was (*repeats his long passionate kiss*), yours — completely. And now, go. And know that it is difficult for me to send you away. (*Hugs her closely to him.*) Oh, my love, my love! (*Brings his head *close to hers and remains sitting a while absorbed in thought.*) Now I am resolved.

WIFE. You are resolved?

CHANCELLOR. And most certainly.

WIFE (*nestling close to him, coquettishly*). Yes? And what is it about, pray? May I know?

CHANCELLOR. There shall be no war.

WIFE (*disappointed*). Oh! I thought you were going to tell me of your love.

CHANCELLOR. And I have made to you the greatest declaration of love. Because I love you so deeply, there will be no war. How could I have gone away from your embraces, with your hot kisses upon my lips, and myself brimming over with love, even as the sea inundates the shore, and sign my name at the bottom of a war-decree, and send forth the children of my people to deeds of blood and enmity? No! No! — Ah — Here come the leaders already. Now go. I'll soon come to you. Come, let me accompany you down a little way.

WIFE (*draws her veil over her face. They go down the stairs.— The four leaders come up.*)

YELLOW. Did you see?

BLACK. With his wife.

YELLOW. With *a woman*. He has time for *her*, but for *us* he is locked in his cabinet. I believe now is the time for us to demand an end to his delays. We are unanimous, the people are restless. He may as well decide. He has no reason to prolong his consideration.

BLACK. We will wait no longer!

BLUE. No! We wait no longer!

GRAY. As long as it's war, let's have it as soon as possible! (*The* CHANCELLOR *returns. The four leaders bow to him. The* CHANCELLOR *replies to them in similar fashion and is about to proceed to his cabinet.*)

YELLOW AND BLACK. Your Excellency!

CHANCELLOR. Gentlemen?

YELLOW. We desire to know the outcome.

BLACK. Where do we stand?

BLUE. War!

GRAY. This way or that, but an end to all this dallying!

CHANCELLOR. You have all spoken. Whom shall I answer?

YELLOW. We all said one and the same thing.

CHANCELLOR. The Gray wants to go " this way or that "—

YELLOW. You know that he never speaks very clearly. He sides with us.

CHANCELLOR. And all of you desire —?

YELLOW. War!

BLACK. A Holy War!

BLUE. War!

GRAY. He — he! War! He — he!

CHANCELLOR (*to the* GRAY). You, too — war?

GRAY. The Turanian is waging war against the Tricker — and we send merchandise to the Tricker — and the Turanian seizes our donkeys.

CHANCELLOR. Well?

GRAY. So we want war! He-he!

Yellow. We have decided that *I* shall be the spokesman.

Chancellor. Shall I not be permitted to speak to whom I wish? But it makes no difference. So then, you insist on war?

Yellow. Most certainly. If we have not yet made clear to you our views, which are the views of the people, then I can make them clearer to you now.

Chancellor. Not necessary.

Yellow. I will be brief.

Chancellor. Was the merchandise that you sent to the Tricker paid for?

Yellow. I'm not talking about the merchandise. But the Turanian seized our donkeys that carried the merchandise.

Chancellor. And therefore, war?

Yellow. Not exactly therefore, but that is a reason.

Chancellor. Oh, I know! I know! The Turanian is becoming too powerful. His wings must be clipped.

Black. He must be converted to our faith.

Blue. Why have we an army, I'd like to know?

Gray. Let it be war, and an end to this uncertainty.

Yellow. Your Excellency, the people are impatient.

Chancellor. You made them impatient.

Yellow. We want to know your decision.

Chancellor. You have already decided for me.

Yellow. Do you agree?

CHANCELLOR. I shall let you know in writing. Everything must be done in orderly fashion and in accordance with the rules.

YELLOW. Why this comedy?

CHANCELLOR (*sternly*). This comedy?

YELLOW. You've come to a decision already — I can see that clearly.

CHANCELLOR. Very well. I'll tell it to you. (*Looks at the leaders sharply and penetratingly, and maintains a prolonged silence as if he took pleasure in trying their patience, their expectancy. Then he speaks in a calm voice.*) There shall be no war.

YELLOW. No war?

BLACK. No war?

BLUE. What?

GRAY. He-he!

YELLOW. The whole nation demands war.—

CHANCELLOR. You criminally talked it into favoring war.

YELLOW. The whole nation cries war and you shall not oppose it.

CHANCELLOR. I am here to rule the nation, not to be ruled by it.

YELLOW. You are here to execute only what the people want and command.

CHANCELLOR. I am here to lead the people and to defend it from misleaders.

YELLOW. You're playing with fire, Your Excellency!

BLUE. Ha-ha!

CHANCELLOR. You threaten me?

YELLOW. The nation wants war and no one can restrain the people from waging it.

CHANCELLOR. The time of your unexpected visit, gentlemen, is up. Go tell the people.—

YELLOW. I'll tell it at once, and if you wish, you may hear how it receives the news from me. (*Hurries to a window, raises it and shouts.*) Hear! Hear! (*A loud commotion is heard in the square, like the din of a tempestuous sea. Cries are distinguished. "Quiet!" . . . "Silence!" . . . Finally the din subsides.*) Hear! The Chancellor has at last decided —(*A loud hurrah arises from the populace.*) Wait! Wait! Listen till I have finished! (*Motions to the crowd to keep still.* BLACK, BLUE *and* GRAY *do likewise.*)

GRAY (*with awkward gestures*). Hush! Hush! Hush! Quiet! Silence! (*Cries from outside.*) "Quiet!" — "Silence!" —

YELLOW. The Chancellor has decreed war — (*Outside the cheering grows louder than ever. Enthusiastic cries are heard: "War! War! War!" The* YELLOW *waves his hands to the crowd, asking for silence.*) No! No! Hear me out!

BLACK (*to the* CHANCELLOR). Do you see?

CHANCELLOR (*laughs scornfully, shaking his head. Outside, cries of "Quiet!" "Silence!"— The din subsides*).

YELLOW (*shouting at the top of his lungs*). War shall not be declared! (*Outside — a dead silence, as if the hearers did not believe their own ears.*)

BLACK (*bends his ear in the direction of the square,*

and raises his finger with deep significance). The calm before the storm.

YELLOW (*shouting*). The Chancellor does not want the war. The Turanian's friendship is more to him than the will of his people. (*A storm of shouts comes from the square.*)

CHANCELLOR. That is provocation! I'll order his arrest!

YELLOW (*shouting*). Come up! The Chancellor is here with us! You can hear it clearly from his own lips!

CHANCELLOR. That is an invitation to bloodshed. The guards outside will use their weapons. You will answer to me for this! The blood will fall upon your own head.

YELLOW. I assume full responsibility. (*Sounds of struggle come from the entrance below, and at length a multitude of* YELLOWS, BLACKS, BLUES *and* GRAYS *rush up the stairs. They advance close to the* CHANCELLOR, *before whom they stand with menacing cries.* "*War! War! War!*" *The doors of the* CHANCELLOR'S *rooms open and his secretaries appear.*)

CHANCELLOR (*to the crowd*). Silence! — Do you think that you will intimidate me with your cries and your tumult? What opinion would you hold of a Chancellor who would let himself be frightened by such a wild onrush and bow to you at once in weak-kneed submission? But you shall not frighten me, and I will carry out what I have decided best for the interests of our land.

THE CROWD (*with an outburst*). War! War! War!

CHANCELLOR. Silence! Remember before whom you stand. If you would speak with me and hear my reply, then cease this shouting and acting like wild beasts.

THE CROWD. War! War! War!

CHANCELLOR. Have you heard my grounds for opposing the war? You know that I have surrendered myself completely to the critical issue, and that for the past twenty-four hours —

YELLOW. Ha-ha-ha!

CHANCELLOR (*furious*). What are you laughing at?

YELLOW (*insolently*). At your twenty-four hours.

CHANCELLOR. What?

YELLOW (*shouting*). He surrendered himself completely here — to a woman!

CHANCELLOR. Scoundrel!

YELLOW. Didn't you see the woman that went down from here before?

VOICES. Yes! Yes! Of course! We saw her! Ha-ha-ha!

CHANCELLOR. Would you have me defend myself against that, too? You all know that my wife — (*With an angry outburst.*) Out of here! Out! Let not a trace of you remain here! I'll call the guards —

VOICES. They're lying downstairs all trampled over, bound hand and foot.

Chancellor. This is revolt! This is revolution!

Yellow. It is the will of the people.

Black. And of God.

Yellow. Sign the proclamation of war, or —

Chancellor (*with an outcry*). I am no longer your Chancellor! Wage the war yourself! Plunge your country into wrack and ruin. Do the people's will — I will not share in it. But I will expose you, and will prove to the people that you imposed your will upon them. I will —

Yellow. This is treason! He is a traitor! He has been bought by the Turanian!

Chancellor. Scoundrel!

Yellow. He abandons the guidance of the nation in such a grave moment and even attempts to incite them against the leaders of the land. What will the enemy say? He will laugh up his sleeve! We are split. We lack unity, and he need not fear us. Now he may do with us as he pleases. Yesterday he seized our donkeys, tomorrow he'll seize our land.— He has been bought by the Turanian!

The Crowd. So that's it? Is that so?

Yellow. You see, he has nothing to say in his defense. His very eyes glow with treason. Aha! That explains why he was seen the night before last with the Turanian's ambassador at the backstairs of his palace!

The Crowd (*looking at each other perplexedly*). Ah! Ah! Ah!

Gray (*placing his heavy hand upon the* Chan-

CELLOR's *shoulder*). So that's the kind of man you are?

BLACK. The traitor must meet a traitor's end!

YELLOW. Lead him out before all our people. Let all the people know what their ruler really was.

VOICES. Lead him out! Lead him out!

GRAY. Come, brother!

BLUE. Clap the fool's cap over his head! String bells around his neck! Traitor!

VOICES. Death to the Traitor! Traitor! Traitor! (*Shouts, jeers, whistling.*)

BLACK. The voice of the people is the voice of God. Amen.

CURTAIN

LITTLE HEROES

A War Episode

PERSONS

A Fourteen-Year-Old Boy
A Thirteen-Year-Old
First Twelve-Year-Old
Second Twelve-Year-Old
An Eleven-Year-Old
A Ten-Year-Old

Time: *The Present.*

Place: *A devastated village in a belligerent and invaded nation.*

LITTLE HEROES

A large living-room in a peasant's house, which has been much damaged by the cannonading. A bomb has crashed through the roof and the ceiling and made a huge hole in the floor. The walls are perforated with bulletholes, the windows smashed, the doors loosened from their hinges. Here and there scattered bits of furniture that has been shot to pieces; only a long sofa and two chairs have escaped destruction.

THE FOURTEEN-YEAR-OLD *enters, looks about him with a rapt, yet angry expression, and stamps his foot. From between his tightly-drawn lips he utters a suppressed cry of scorn, points a menacing fist at the shattered windows and the wall at the rear, as if at an enemy in the distance, on whom he would wreak vengeance.*

FIRST TWELVE-YEAR-OLD (*appears at the door, and stops in consternation*). Oh! This is worse than at my house!

THE FOURTEEN-YEAR-OLD. Where are they all?

FIRST TWELVE-YEAR-OLD. I don't know. Didn't see 'em. (*Enters, looks into the hole in the floor, then at the gap in the ceiling.*) Right through.

You can see the sky. That must have been a giant bomb! — Where did it strike your mother?

THE FOURTEEN-YEAR-OLD. Where? Everywhere at once! She was simply torn to shreds.

FIRST TWELVE-YEAR-OLD. I mean, what part of the house was she in when it came?

THE FOURTEEN-YEAR-OLD. She was standing right here near the closet.

FIRST TWELVE-YEAR-OLD. And the closet was smashed, too?

THE FOURTEEN-YEAR-OLD. Can't you see? Knocked to bits!

FIRST TWELVE-YEAR-OLD (*looking about*). All the furniture! (*Sees the sofa, and thumps it here and there with his fist, as if testing its strength.*) At my house, too —

THE FOURTEEN-YEAR-OLD (*interrupting, with a touch of scorn*). I know. Didn't I see? . . . Hardly a thing touched, no damage at all.

FIRST TWELVE-YEAR-OLD. Why! A whole wall was crushed, and our chimney, and the shed burned down, and our dog was killed and his kennel shot to pieces, and grandma died of fright.

THE FOURTEEN-YEAR-OLD (*looking out of the window*). They must have started a game of ball.

FIRST TWELVE-YEAR-OLD. Nobody plays ball these days.

THE FOURTEEN-YEAR-OLD. Well, something else, then.

FIRST TWELVE-YEAR-OLD. Nobody plays anything at all now. I play all by myself. I feel so sad. I hide behind the house and play marbles.

THE FOURTEEN-YEAR-OLD. You big baby!

FIRST TWELVE-YEAR-OLD. I'm not a baby! But I feel so sad, and I'm awfully hungry, too. Haven't you a crumb of bread around here?

THE FOURTEEN-YEAR-OLD. Ruins, that's what we've got.

FIRST TWELVE-YEAR-OLD. They went to the enemy to ask for bread.

THE FOURTEEN-YEAR-OLD. What a disgrace!

FIRST TWELVE-YEAR-OLD. They're all so hungry. Aren't you hungry?

THE FOURTEEN-YEAR-OLD. I won't touch the enemy's bread!

FIRST TWELVE-YEAR-OLD. Your father hasn't been killed yet in the war. My father was shot in the stomach. (*Turns to the* THIRTEEN-YEAR-OLD *and the* SECOND TWELVE-YEAR-OLD, *who have just come in*). Just see how the cannon shot right through the ceiling and through the floor!

THE FOURTEEN-YEAR-OLD (*to the new arrivals*). And that's what you call coming right away?

THE THIRTEEN-YEAR-OLD (*gazing into the hole*). Ooh! What a hole!

SECOND TWELVE-YEAR-OLD. What a shot that must have been!

FIRST TWELVE-YEAR-OLD. Right through and through. And tore his mother to bits. And smashed all the furniture. Just look at the pieces!

THE THIRTEEN-YEAR-OLD (*taking a seat upon the sofa*). I had to stay with my little sister. She won't stop crying, she's so hungry. I put my finger in her mouth. My! How she sucked it!

SECOND TWELVE-YEAR-OLD. My mother has one fainting-spell after another. I had to steal away.

THE ELEVEN-YEAR-OLD (*enters, holding the* TEN-YEAR-OLD *by the hand*). Bah! I could barely drag along with him to take care of.

THE TEN-YEAR-OLD. Why should I run? To get more hungry?

THE ELEVEN-YEAR-OLD. Ooh my! What a hole!

THE TEN-YEAR-OLD. If it rains, it'll rain in.

THE THIRTEEN-YEAR-OLD. You don't say so. (*To the* FOURTEEN-YEAR-OLD, *who is excited, and paces back and forth amid the ruins.*) You've called together a regular meeting!

THE FOURTEEN-YEAR-OLD. That's just what. I have a plan, and I need helpers.

THE THIRTEEN-YEAR-OLD (*stretching out at full length upon the sofa*). He has a plan and he needs helpers.

THE ELEVEN-YEAR-OLD (*sits down at the edge of the hole in the floor and dangles his feet within*). What a big hole!

FIRST TWELVE-YEAR-OLD (*sits down beside the* ELEVEN-YEAR-OLD).

SECOND TWELVE-YEAR-OLD (*about to follow suit, but changes his mind and takes a chair*).

THE TEN-YEAR-OLD (*lies down on the floor, his head pillowed against a pile of débris*).

THE FOURTEEN-YEAR-OLD (*passionately*).

Aren't we now the only men left in the village? The old folks are only old folks, after all. They can't march. Can't fight. If it comes to a battle, what good are they? And the women are only women. They're certainly not men. And the girls surely ain't men, either. So we're the only men! Are we going to stand by like the little girls and keep on playing with dolls?

FIRST TWELVE-YEAR-OLD. They aren't playing with dolls now. They're crying.

THE FOURTEEN-YEAR-OLD. Well, are we going to sit and cry? Are we going to be 'fraid-cats and cry-babies? We're young boys, fellows, men. Isn't that so?

THE TEN-YEAR-OLD. Sure. But I want to eat.

THE FOURTEEN-YEAR-OLD. The enemy is coming further and further into our country. Our army is retreating before it. The enemy is capturing one village after the other; one city after another. Soon he'll take over our whole nation altogether. So that we've got to do something about it! Is that right, or not!

THE ELEVEN-YEAR-OLD. Sure it's right!

THE THIRTEEN-YEAR-OLD. And what shall we do?

SECOND TWELVE-YEAR-OLD. I've counted thirty-seven bullet-holes in the wall.

THE FOURTEEN-YEAR-OLD. Aren't we to the rear of the enemy? Isn't that so? Aren't we behind their lines?

THE ELEVEN-YEAR-OLD. Naturally we're behind

their lines. They've already marched thirty miles further into the country.

THE FOURTEEN-YEAR-OLD. Then we can do a good deal against them.

THE ELEVEN-YEAR-OLD (*diffidently*). Naturally. A good deal.

THE THIRTEEN-YEAR-OLD. One speaks and the other repeats, just like a parrot.

THE ELEVEN-YEAR-OLD (*more firmly and boldly*). Naturally! A good deal!

SECOND TWELVE-YEAR-OLD. My! What a shot that must have been! Bang! Through the roof, the ceiling, the floor! Whizz!

THE TEN-YEAR-OLD. Near us, too, there was —

THE FOURTEEN-YEAR-OLD (*to the* THIRTEEN-YEAR-OLD, *vehemently*). Can you shinney up a high pole?

THE THIRTEEN-YEAR-OLD. Better than you.

FIRST TWELVE-YEAR-OLD. So can I. Just like a cat.

THE ELEVEN-YEAR-OLD. I can do it better than all of you.

THE FOURTEEN-YEAR-OLD. Then one of us is to climb up a telegraph pole and cut the wires.

THE THIRTEEN-YEAR-OLD. Mm! But you're extravagant!

THE FOURTEEN-YEAR-OLD. We'll go out three together, or four. That's why I need helpers.

THE THIRTEEN-YEAR-OLD. Don't forget that at every telegraph pole there's a soldier with a gun.

THE FOURTEEN-YEAR-OLD (*taking a sharp knife*

from under his coat). And what's this for, then? (*The youthful group stares at the knife*).

The Eleven-Year-Old. We've got a nice big kitchen-knife, too.

The Ten-Year-Old. But we've got nothing to cut with it.

The Fourteen-Year-Old. You're all of you to provide yourselves with knives like this, and at night, when it's pitch dark, we're to crawl, on our bellies, up behind the guard, stab him in the heart, climb up the pole and cut the wires.

The Eleven-Year-Old. Here's how we'll do it. (*Crawls carefully over the floor.*) And then, Zip! (*Makes a violent thrust into the air, as if into an enemy.*) Then, up the pole, up, up. (*Springs up from the floor and imitates climbing.*)

The Ten-Year-Old. And on the murdered soldier we'll find some bread.

The Thirteen-Year-Old. But supposing the soldier sees us or hears us?

The Fourteen-Year-Old. He mustn't see us or hear us. We'll do it quietly, ever so quietly.

The Ten-Year-Old. I can crawl as softly — as a worm. And I'll take our big sharp knife — but I'm awfully hungry. I want to eat!

The Thirteen-Year-Old. And a soldier wears thick clothes!

Second Twelve-Year-Old. They wear armor. That's what they say. Made out of tin. On their chests. So that a bullet can't go through.

First Twelve-Year-Old. Well then, we'll aim

our knives at their stomachs, or their necks, or their eyes.

The Eleven-Year-Old. We could even stab one in the knee. Crawl up quietly, so quietly and — slash! Right into his knee, so that his foot'll come off.

The Fourteen-Year-Old. Exactly. And make a good job of it. Just let him fall, badly wounded, and we'll make an end of him.

The Ten-Year-Old. And take all his food away from him.

The Fourteen-Year-Old. In that way we can kill a good many guards and cut a good deal of telegraph and telephone wires. That'll help our soldiers.

The Eleven-Year-Old. The less soldiers the enemy has, the better for our side.

The Fourteen-Year-Old. And with all the telegraph and telephone wires cut, the enemy won't know where in the world he is.

The Eleven-Year-Old. And then our men will give the enemy such a beating, that he won't know what's happening to him. And then he'll run away.

The Ten-Year-Old. And we'll have lots of bread again.

Second Twelve-Year-Old. The enemy has heaps of food. Did you see all the provision wagons go by? I counted forty-four. And did you see that big field-kitchen?

The Ten-Year-Old (*utters a brief sigh, as if the*

field-kitchen and the provision-wagons had inspired savory recollections).

THE FOURTEEN-YEAR-OLD (*trembling with emotion*). But all that is nothing. We can do much more. (*Looks around, to see whether some eavesdropper be listening, and then continues in tones of secrecy.*) In the nobleman's house the enemy's commander-in-chief has made his headquarters. He has in his possession all the enemy's plans. We'll steal into the house — at midnight — when he's fast asleep — kill him and steal his plans. Once that's accomplished, then it's all up with the enemy.

THE ELEVEN-YEAR-OLD. My! My! But that's a crackerjack scheme!

FIRST TWELVE-YEAR-OLD (*in glee*). Gee! The commander-in-chief! — To kill him —(*Embraces the* ELEVEN-YEAR-OLD *and together they roll around joyously*).

THE THIRTEEN-YEAR-OLD (*with ironic laughter*). Ha, ha! They're going to murder the commander-in-chief! Why, he's surrounded by generals and officers and soldiers!

THE FOURTEEN-YEAR-OLD. Makes no difference. That's what we must do.

THE THIRTEEN-YEAR-OLD. First prove that you can steal up behind a guard at a telegraph pole!

THE FOURTEEN-YEAR-OLD. We certainly will.

THE ELEVEN-YEAR-OLD. You bet!

THE THIRTEEN-YEAR-OLD. Then you'll all be in heaven soon, that's all I say.

THE FOURTEEN-YEAR-OLD. You're a common coward, that's what you are!

THE THIRTEEN-YEAR-OLD. You mean I'm smarter than you; that's what you mean.

THE FOURTEEN-YEAR-OLD. You're a traitor!

THE ELEVEN-YEAR-OLD. The betrayer! We ought to kill him altogether.

THE THIRTEEN-YEAR-OLD. I'm no traitor! I'm hungry, that's all I am! I want to eat! I haven't had a bite in two days.

THE FOURTEEN-YEAR-OLD. I'm just as hungry as you. We're all hungry.

SECOND TWELVE-YEAR-OLD. My mother keeps on fainting from hunger. Yesterday she gave us the last piece of bread in the house. She herself hasn't eaten for two days. But I'm fearfully hungry, just the same.

FIRST TWELVE-YEAR-OLD. I'm terribly hungry, too. But I don't pay any attention to it.

THE ELEVEN-YEAR-OLD. Neither do I. I turn my tongue in my mouth and chew it. And it feels just like eating. (*Pointing to the* TEN-YEAR-OLD.) I told him to do it, too.

THE TEN-YEAR-OLD. My tongue can't turn any more. (*Whimpering.*) I want to eat.

THE FOURTEEN-YEAR-OLD. We are all hungry. Just the same we can do something for our side.

THE THIRTEEN-YEAR-OLD (*succumbing to tears, and rubbing his palms over his chest and his stomach*). I'm hungry. My insides — are so hollow — and I feel so faint. I'll die of hunger.

THE TEN-YEAR-OLD (*breaks into tears, sobbing*).

THE ELEVEN-YEAR-OLD (*slapping him*). There he goes! Crying! (*Begins whimpering himself.*) Cry-baby! Cry-baby!

SECOND TWELVE-YEAR-OLD. My mother'll die of hunger. Perhaps she's dead already. (*Bursts into tears.*)

FIRST TWELVE-YEAR-OLD (*tearfully*). I'm getting hungry myself now. I wasn't paying any attention to it, but now they made me hungry. (*Sinks down to the floor and weeps. All except the* FOURTEEN-YEAR-OLD *are now crying. Deep, restrained sobs betray their inconsolable misery.*)

THE FOURTEEN-YEAR-OLD. They're all crying! Just look at them, there — the cry-babies! A fine lot you are to accomplish anything with! Stop it! Stop crying, I say! Oh! (*Brandishes his knife as if he would gladly stab some one, finally flings it vehemently away, sinks into the empty chair, hiding his face in his arm, and his sobs are soon heard with those of the others*).

CURTAIN

THE BEAUTIFUL NUN

A Drama in One Act

[Written in June, 1919]

PERSONS

The Abbess
Sister Ernestina
Sister Audacia
Sister Hedwig
First Soldier
Second Soldier

The action takes place in time of war

THE BEAUTIFUL NUN

The small chapel of a nunnery. Before the image of the Holy Virgin burns the perpetual lamp; at the foot of the image kneel the ABBESS *and* SISTERS ERNESTINA *and* AUDACIA.—*From without comes the booming of cannon.*

ABBESS. Holy Virgin, count it not as a sin against us that none of the sisters could be found to risk her life and her honor, and remain here to tend the perpetual lamp. How gladly would I myself stay behind, were it not my duty to lead all the sisters to safety. You know that I would willingly have done so,— you who see deep into our hearts. And you would guard me here, you would have warded me from all evil, and no harm would befall me. (*Crosses herself and arises.*)

THE SISTERS (*arise*).

ABBESS. Will none of you then remain under the secure protection of our Holy Virgin? Sister Ernestina, you who are so old in years and strong in faith?

SISTER ERNESTINA. Gladly would I remain here. I know that the burden of years is a great protection for a lone woman, and surely the hand of the Holy Mother is an even greater protection. But who knows the savage enemy in all his godlessness and wantonness? He acknowledges neither God nor the Holy Mother, nor does he recognize age. I should not wish my many years to be sullied by criminal lust. Pardon me, mother, and let me go with you.

ABBESS. I can only say that you are childish and that God is not strong within you, Sister Ernestina. I will not force you to remain here. Force is an evil service to the Lord. The Holy Mother asks only love; she would be served by love. Will you not show her that love-service, Sister Audacia? You may assume the office and remain here in all security. You know how very ugly you are. And your ugliness, together with God's help, will furnish you even greater protection.

AUDACIA. I know that I have ever thanked God I was not born with the proud heart that comes from the beautiful face. But never did I know I was as ugly as all that.

ABBESS. I wish I had a mirror here. If you could see how you look now you would yourself fall in a swoon and for many a day be unable to take a crumb in your mouth for nausea. You came to the nunnery to hide from the sight of a mirror.

AUDACIA. Beauty is always merely a matter of taste. How do you know the taste of the enemy's soldiery?

ABBESS. Fie! You must not remain here. You will beam with pride if the beasts attack you.

AUDACIA. You should not say that. Can you not see that I desire to leave?

ABBESS. Yes. Talk is useless.— Holy Mother!

(*Crosses herself piously.* ERNESTINA *and* AUDACIA *do likewise. Then they all turn toward the door.*)

SISTER HEDWIG (*appears in the doorway. She is very beautiful. The modest nun's garb enhances her beauty*).

ABBESS (*unable to suppress a cry of amazement*). Sister Hedwig, what are you doing here? You should have been among the first to leave. Why have you brought your beauty here? Be off at once! The enemy is already before the gates.

HEDWIG (*entering the chapel*). I will remain here.

ABBESS. What?

ERNESTINA *and* AUDACIA (*cross themselves*).

HEDWIG. I will remain here to guard the church and to tend the perpetual lamp.

ABBESS. Are you in your right senses, sister?

ERNESTINA. She is certainly out of her mind.

AUDACIA. That comes from her great beauty, which all have praised so much that her head has been turned.

HEDWIG. You have read it aright, Sister Audacia. It comes to me from my great beauty, but not because my head has been turned. God sees my heart, and you should all have learned by now that my beauty has never been a source of pride to me. Yet I will remain here, because I rely upon our Holy Mother and — upon my beauty.

ABBESS. What do you mean?

HEDWIG. My beauty will be my shield.

ABBESS. Child! What are you saying!

HEDWIG. They will not dare to stain my beauty.

ABBESS. Folly!

HEDWIG. The Holy Mother sent me that thought. I know that the inspiration comes from the Holy Virgin.

AUDACIA. That comes from Satan. Holy Mother, forgive her her words!

HEDWIG. Beauty wakes piety. You have looked upon many a holy picture in your life; did you ever behold an ugly one? How does our Christ look? How does our Holy Mother appear? How she moves us with her divine beauty! How do the angels appear? Beauty is inspiration, beauty is prayer, beauty is religion.

ABBESS. Beauty is seduction, beauty is temptation, beauty is intoxicating wine. Why do you speak, sister, of pictures and statues, of cold marble and colors upon dead canvas? You will be a living, beautiful nun among lust-driven soldiers of the enemy.

HEDWIG. They will not touch me.

ABBESS. They will. . . . (*Men's voices heard from without.*) Ah, they are already here! . . . Quickly, quickly! . . . Sister Hedwig! Sister Hedwig! (*Dashes out, followed by* SISTERS ERNESTINA *and* AUDACIA.)

HEDWIG (*slowly approaches the image and sinks to her knees*).

TWO SOLDIERS (*dash in with bayonets fixed; seeing nobody, they halt and lower their weapons*).

FIRST SOLDIER (*crosses himself*).

SECOND SOLDIER (*about to do the same, but drops his hand*). Bah! An enemy church!

FIRST SOLDIER. Just look! A nun! On her knees!

SECOND SOLDIER. She is calling down destruction upon us there. We'll give it to her! Let's see whether she's a young one.

HEDWIG (*crosses herself and hides her face in her hands*).

FIRST SOLDIER. She has concealed her face. That means she's a young one.

SECOND SOLDIER. You can tell that from her figure. No old worshipper would have a figure like that. Appetizing, what?

FIRST SOLDIER. But if she's remained behind without fear, then she must be an ugly hag.

SECOND SOLDIER (*approaching* HEDWIG). You've prayed long enough. Let's have a look at you.

HEDWIG (*removes her hands from her face and crosses herself*).

SECOND SOLDIER (*recoils in surprise*).

HEDWIG (*rises slowly to her feet and turns her face toward the soldiers; she stands close to the wall before the image, and her countenance wears a calm, pious, forgiving expression*).

FIRST SOLDIER (*breathless with amazement*). What a beauty! As if she had stepped down from a picture.

SECOND SOLDIER. And she wasn't afraid. Remarkable. Was she forgotten in the flight, or was she purposely left behind?

HEDWIG. I desired to remain here.

BOTH SOLDIERS (*are entranced with her voice*).

SECOND SOLDIER (*after a brief pause*). You desired to remain behind, did you?

HEDWIG. To perform my religious duties.

SECOND SOLDIER. And weren't at all afraid?

HEDWIG. I am not afraid.

SECOND SOLDIER. Not afraid, hey?

HEDWIG. I am not in danger.

SECOND. What? (*Both soldiers look around them.*)

HEDWIG. You misunderstood me. No one is concealed hereabouts to protect me. My protection is in you yourselves.

SECOND SOLDIER. You don't say!

HEDWIG. You will allow me to continue my worship before the Holy Virgin and to say my prayers. You, too, are Christians?

SECOND SOLDIER. That makes no difference. I don't know yet whether you remained behind because you were such a pious Christian. Why *did* you remain behind?

HEDWIG. To guard the perpetual lamp.

SECOND SOLDIER. Couldn't some old carcass have been left for that purpose?

HEDWIG. They were all afraid.

SECOND SOLDIER. All the old frights were afraid, and you felt no fear?

HEDWIG. No.

SECOND SOLDIER. There must be something behind all this. This is a trick.

HEDWIG. I am the only soul in all the nunnery.

SECOND SOLDIER. Aren't you supposed to discover something here? To do a little spying?

HEDWIG (*shakes her head in denial, sincerely and piously*).

SECOND SOLDIER (*seizes her arm, near the shoulder*). Are you speaking the truth?

HEDWIG (*looks at him with a calm, pious, piercing glance*).

SECOND SOLDIER (*laughs embarrassedly and releases her*).

FIRST SOLDIER. She looks like a living Madonna. . . . You could almost believe that the Holy Virgin had stepped down from the image. . . . Ha, ha. . . .

HEDWIG (*shakes her head*). No. I am only a nun — a servant to the Holy Virgin.

SECOND SOLDIER (*to the* FIRST SOLDIER). A curse on you. You almost scared me, you jackass!

HEDWIG. But it was the will of the Holy Mother that I should remain here.

SECOND SOLDIER. If not the will of somebody else. None of your idle talk, now. Such a beautiful maiden should not have been left behind. We are hungry soldiers. Hungry for everything, do you understand! For a woman, and a young and beautiful one in the bargain — over-hungry. You should have expected that.

FIRST SOLDIER. Ha, ha. . . . And *so* hungry!

HEDWIG. You will not disturb me in my duties. Go in peace.

SECOND SOLDIER. Indeed! (*Raises his gun, aims, and shoots down the perpetual lamp.*)

HEDWIG (*shudders, crosses herself and murmurs a prayer*).

FIRST SOLDIER. Ahhhhh. . . . Ha, ha!

SECOND SOLDIER. There goes your duty! What will you say now?

HEDWIG (*still stands with eyes closed, her face expressing anguish and grief*).

SECOND SOLDIER (*to the* FIRST SOLDIER). A beauty, hey?

FIRST SOLDIER. Devilish beautiful.

SECOND SOLDIER. She appeals to you, hey?

FIRST SOLDIER. Appeals! I should say so, to the deuce with you!

SECOND SOLDIER. Then what can hold us back?

HEDWIG (*opens her eyes wide and stares at them*).

FIRST SOLDIER. When she stands looking at us like that?

SECOND SOLDIER. You're a coward,— a timorous rabbit!

FIRST SOLDIER. God knows I'm not.

SECOND SOLDIER. And you're afraid of her.

FIRST SOLDIER. And you're no braver.

SECOND SOLDIER. Ha, ha!

FIRST SOLDIER. Women with faces like that may be attacked only in the dark.

SECOND SOLDIER. Ha, ha! You're an ass! (*Harshly, to* HEDWIG.) What are you standing there for, as if you were glued to the wall? You've no more duties to perform here; there's no perpetual lamp to tend now. You may go!

HEDWIG. I will get another lamp, light it, and pray for your sins.

SECOND SOLDIER. Wait a while; I will add a few so that you can pray for the new ones, too. Well, why don't you go for the lamp? Why don't you stir from your place? — If I take the notion into my head to attack you, I'll have no fear, even if you stand there looking at me through those big eyes of yours. Do you understand? — You needn't look at me like that! Understand? The mistake is all yours, and you have nobody else to blame.— Well, why don't you say something? What are you standing there for, staring like that — as if you were glued to the wall? — Hey! Isn't there something behind you there on the wall? Aren't you concealing something? A button? A signal to press? Away from that wall!

HEDWIG (*raises both her hands*). I swear to you by the Holy Mother of God . . .

SECOND SOLDIER (*breathing hard and eyeing her like a wild beast, awaiting the propitious moment to attack her; he maneuvers so as to get behind her*).

HEDWIG (*sees his plan and strives to keep him continually before her eyes*).

FIRST SOLDIER (*as Hedwig turns her back to him, smiles bashfully and then throws himself upon her from behind, with both hands across her face, crying out wildly*).

Second Soldier (*with a beastly roar raises* Hedwig *from the ground, seizing her by the legs*).

CURTAIN

POLAND — 1919

" A Scene Out of Terrible Days "

POLAND — 1919

SCENE

A spacious, dark cellar. From somewhere in the background there steals in a sunbeam, announcing that the clear sun of daylight reigns outside, and revealing the silhouettes of various persons that people the cellar. Most of the forms lie huddled together upon the earth; it is difficult to recognize them as human shapes. A few are seated; three men stand about the shaft of sunlight; one on each side, close to the wall; the third before it, his hands crossed on his breast and his face toward the light. On the ground, in the triangle formed by the three standing men, a group of little boys and girls, reading from books.

Silence. The atmosphere quivers with intense strain. All are listening intently to every sound that comes from outside. For an appreciable while the silence is unbroken. Then commences a conversation between those who are seated and those who are lying upon the ground. There is a whispering of dry, hungering, weary voices, with pauses between the queries and the replies.

VOICES.

— It is still quiet outside.

— How long has it been quiet?

— She speaks of time! Do we even know how long we have been here?

— It's surely three or four hours that it's been so quiet.

— What can it mean?

— Have they ceased fighting, or —?

— It seems as if they've started to parley. There's not a sound from any quarter.

THE MAN AT THE RIGHT OF THE SUNBEAM. How does our night-prayer run? "To my right, Archangel Michael; to my left, Archangel Gabriel; before me, Archangel Uriel; behind me, Archangel Rafæl. . . ." And what have we now? — to our left, the Poles; to our right, the Ukrainians; before us, the Russians; behind, the Rumanians. . . .

THE MAN AT THE LEFT (*ironically*). And where is God?

ONE WHO IS SEATED. If we had thought of God before, then perhaps we should be better off now.

THE MAN AT THE LEFT. How much better off, dear Rabbi? When has the goodness and the piety of the Jews ever availed them?

VOICES.

— The Jews have always been scapegoats.

— Outside there, they'll all make peace and then fall upon us all at once.

— One against the other, and all against us.

— We aid in all wars, and then we're massacred even by those in whose ranks we have fought.

— Who knows what will yet be our fate?

— Woe! Woe! (*There rise the sounds of a soft, guarded, exhausted, dry weeping, for they have wept out all their tears.*)

A Woman, Seated. Oh, Lord of the universe. Let them do anything, anything. . . . Let them break my bones, let them twist my arms, let them kill me; but not that, not that. . . .

A Man (*beside her*). It was fifteen years ago I heard you say that for the first time.

The Woman. And how many times have I repeated it since!

Another Woman. Many a Jewish daughter prayed that before her; and many a one will pray it after her, perhaps. (*Groans.*)

A Man Who is Standing (*he is at the right, near the wall, and is invisible because of the intense darkness; his voice is stifled, hoarse, and echoes with despair.*) Why? Why?

The Voice of a Maiden (*weakly, as if from underground*). Wasn't that a chill breeze that just blew through?

Silence

A Little Boy (*near the sunbeam*). I've finished my book. Now I'll get very hungry.

A Little Girl (*near him*). Let's change books. I'll give you mine.

The Boy. What are you reading?

The Girl. A Polish book.

The Boy. I don't know Polish. I'll get terribly hungry.

THE GIRL. Then I'll teach it to you.

THE BOY. Oh, yes! Good-d-d! Then I won't be so awfully hungry. (*They both stretch out upon the ground, before the shaft of light.*)

THE MAN AT THE RIGHT. Just look at the "People of the Book"— And some Polish rioter will come along and smash their heads against a rock.

THE VOICE OF THE MAIDEN. I'm so cold.

Silence

THE MAN FACING THE SUNBEAM. But outside it's a glorious summer's day. The sun shines and laughs and warms and —

ONE WHO IS LYING DOWN. Shows where to shoot.

THE MAN FACING THE SUNLIGHT. Yet we are fortunate to have at least one ray of sunlight with us.

THE VOICE OF THE MAIDEN. What would I do if it were light here? I am all naked. Will no one cover me with something?

Silence

VOICES.

— The silence, it seems, is even worse than the firing. While the shooting was going on we could at least expect a bomb to strike the place and put an end to everything. Now we are utterly at a loss.

— Such silence is terror.

— It seems that they are planning some horrible thing around this house.

— God forbid!

A Little Boy. I'd like to crawl out and take a look around.

His Mother. Lie where you are!

The Boy. They couldn't see me. I'd creep like a worm.

His Mother. He'd creep, he says! He can hardly move a hand.

The Boy. I'm small, and they couldn't see me.

His Mother (*sternly*). Lie where you are!

The Boy (*petulantly*). I'm hungry!

The Voice of a Woman (*very weak*). A crumb of bread. . . . A crumb of bread. . . .

The Voice of the Maiden. I can forget my hunger, but not my nakedness. If I only had something to wrap about me.

One Ill with Fever (*with an outcry*). I'm burning! I'm on fire!—(*His mouth is stopped.— Some women begin to sob softly.*)

The Unseen Questioner (*as if groaning*). Why? Why?

One Who is Seated. It's enough to lift off your head.

Another. Mine has already flown off. Like the cover of a kettle.— Whizz!— Up flew my skull-bone; up, up, and after it my very brains. I can see it high up there. And if I should want to reach it, I would need a very high ladder. That's what makes me so sad. I haven't any such ladder.

A Child (*begins to cry in a very weak voice*). I want my fireman's ladder.

The Mother. Hush-sh! . . .

A WOMAN. The poor thing is starving and asks for toys.

THE MOTHER (*herself beginning to weep*). Hush-sh! . . .

Silence

THE MAN FACING THE SUNBEAM. How the sun's ray calls and beckons to us! It makes us forget everything. It seems as if I could mount it and journey upward and upward. . . . And verses of happiness fill my mind. Why do I see only green fields outside? And a merry, glorious world? And a happy tranquility.

VOICES.

— A "happy tranquility" indeed!

— We ought really to find out what's going on.

THE LITTLE BOY. I'll crawl out.

VOICES.

— We should all crawl out. Why remain in hiding? Why torture ourselves? Let them wipe us out, and end it all.

— As long as we draw breath, we prefer to live.

— Rather a slow exhaustion in hopes of remaining alive, than the certainty of death.

THE LITTLE BOY. I'd crawl upon my belly. I wouldn't even raise my head. I'd peek just like this.

THE RABBI. We'll wait through just this day. And if it still remains quiet outside, one of us will have to crawl out and discover how matters stand.

A MAN (*his voice is scarcely audible*). I'll not survive this day. I am done for.

Silence

The Voice of a Woman. A crumb of bread. . . . A crumb of bread. . . .

Voices.

— Soon we'll all be speaking like that.

— We, too, will forget our names for hunger.

— We'll never leave this place alive.

— What will not be eaten up by the lice, will be devoured by the mice.

— It's enough to lift your head off.

The Madman. We'll stand upon one another's shoulders and reach the head.

A Woman (*sits bending over something in her lap, and groans with stifling despair*). Gone! . . . Gone! . . . He's dead! . . . My child is dead! . . . Tseitele, Avrahmele, Layzer'l is dead. . . . Your brother is dead.

Two Children (*seated beside her, burst into tears, weeping with weak voices*).

The Woman. He is dead. Now he is well; now he is happy. . . .

Voices.

— Ah! Lord of the universe!

— Where can we bury him?

— He'll not be the only corpse very long; we'll all soon join him.

— We'll have to crawl out of here. How can we stay now?

— We'll have to dig a deep grave here.

— For all of us.

A LITTLE BOY (*wailing*). I'm afraid! I want to go out! (*A hand is pressed against his mouth.*)

THE QUESTIONER (*with an outburst of tears*). Why? Why?

ONE WHO IS SEATED. Because we meddle in everything. Because we have a hand in everything. For our revolutions.

THE MAN AT THE LEFT OF THE SUNBEAM. Because of your money-grubbing. Because of your exploitation. Because of your capitalism.

THE RABBI. Because we have forgotten God.

ONE WHO IS SEATED. Because of our aloofness. Because of our attitude as the chosen people.

THE MAN AT THE RIGHT OF THE SUNBEAM. Because of your fawning; because of your assimilation. Because of your obtrusiveness.

A WOMAN. Now they start to argue. Found the right time for it. They'll get to shrieking yet.

VOICES.

— Better let us dig the little grave.

— With what can we dig it?

— I believe I'm lying upon a spade.

— Who has the strength to dig?

THE WOMAN. I myself. I myself will dig the grave, and dig it for two. How long can I last? I hope I last long enough to dig the grave.

HER TWO CHILDREN (*burst into tears*).

THE WOMAN. I'll dig it for four. Don't cry. I'll dig it for four. (*Arises and drags herself in the direction of the voice that has mentioned the spade.*)

THE VOICE. You will have to remove the spade yourself from under me. I haven't the strength to stir.

THE WOMAN (*pulls forth the spade, returns to her place and begins to dig.— The sobbing of women is heard*).

THE VOICE OF THE MAIDEN. If she would only scatter the thrown-up earth over me. It would cover my nakedness.

THE UNSEEN QUESTIONER (*through clenched teeth and in an angry voice*). Why? Why? (*Silence. Only the digging is heard; here and there a weak groan; here and there a sob.*)

A LITTLE BOY. I can't read any more. My eyes hurt.

ANOTHER. My eyes hurt, too. But when it gets real dark, then we won't be able to read. And then we'll get terribly hungry.

A LITTLE GIRL. When it grows dark we'll go to sleep.

FIRST BOY. You must lie down on your stomach, and press it hard. Then you won't feel hungry.

THE SECOND. When I lie on my stomach I lick up the earth, and I get such an unpleasant feeling. . . .

THE VOICE OF A WOMAN. A crumb of bread. . . . A crumb of bread. . . .

ONE ILL WITH FEVER. I'm burning! . . . I'm on fire; . . . I . . . (*a hand is clapped over his mouth*) on fire!

The Voice of the Maiden. And I'm so cold. I'm freezing. . . . And how shall I get out of this place? I'm totally naked.

Voices.

— She actually hopes to get out of here!

— There's no getting out of this place.

— Death is lurking about. . . . Madness is hovering around. . . . They are crawling over us like vermin. . . . I would swear that there's a dead body next to me. . . .

— Woe! Woe! (*Weeping.*)

The Woman (*who is digging*). When I get through I'll give you the spade.

The Questioner (*with a sudden outcry*). Why?

Voices (*they come from various directions, and ring with terror*). Hush-sh!

One Not Far from the Questioner. We have forgotten how to shriek. That is it. When the Romans started to rend the skin from the face of Rabbi Ishmael the High Priest,— one of the ten martyrs slain by the authorities,— he let out such piercing shrieks that there came a voice from heaven, saying: "If you shriek once more, I'll wreck the entire world." That's how we ought to be able to shriek to-day, and let the whole world crumble to dust!

The Poet (*facing the sunbeam*). No! Outside shines the glorious sun! Vast and round and brilliant!

The Man at the Right. And its rays tell us of a land whither the Jews shall return.— it tells of full freedom, of a home of their own, of sunny independence, of a life without persecution, without scorn, without pogroms, of a life —

THE MAN AT THE LEFT. Without master or slave, without exploiter and exploited. The sunbeam speaks to us of a new day and a new world, with a new justice, new relations between man and man, between people and people.

THE POET. Then let us saddle the sunbeam and fare forth upon its back into the sunny world. For this is the ray of hope. This is the —

(*A bomb strikes the spot, burying the refugees beneath the ruins. But above the débris, in the bright light of day, are visible the* POET *and the* QUESTIONER, *gasping with their last breath.*)

THE POET (*in exaltation, dying*). The vast, beautiful, glorious sun!

THE QUESTIONER (*with a terrible, heaven-rending outcry*). Why? Why?

CURTAIN

THE STRANGER

A Legend-Drama

THE LEGEND IN THE MIDRASH

Rabbi Yudan, son of Rabbi Aibu, said: Menahem is his (the Messiah's) name. This was the statement made by Rabbi Yudan, son of Rabbi Aibu: Once upon a time a man was plowing, when one of his oxen began to cry aloud. An Arab happened to pass by and said to him, "Who are you?" And he replied, "I am a Jew." And the Arab said, "Unyoke your oxen." The Jew asked, "Why?" The other replied, "Because the Temple has been destroyed." Whereupon the Jew asked, "How do you know that?" And the other answered, "I know it from the crying of your ox." As the Arab spoke to him thus the ox again cried out. And the Arab said to the Jew, "Put your oxen back into harness, for there has been born the redeemer of the Jews." Whereupon the first asked, "What is his name?" And the Arab answered, "Menahem is his name." "And what is the name of his father?" He answered, "Hezekiah." And the first asked, "Where does he dwell?" The other answered, "In the Arab district of Bethlehem, in Judah."

And the man sold his oxen and his plow and bought linens for children, and wandered from one town to another, from one land to another, until he came thither. All the village women came to buy of his wares, but the woman who was the mother of the child did not buy of him. So he said to her, " Why do you not buy linens for your child? " And she answered, " Because my child's fate is an evil one." And he asked, " Why? " Whereupon she replied, " Because at his birth the Temple was destroyed." He answered, however, " We must trust in the Lord of the world; through him was the Temple destroyed, and through him will it be rebuilt. Take some of these children's linens," he counseled, " and after some days I shall come for the money." So she took some and went away.

Days passed and the man said, " I'll go and learn how the child is getting along." So he went to her and asked, " How is the child getting on? " And she replied, " Didn't I tell you that his fate was an evil one and pursued him? For since that time winds and storms came and carried him off." Whereupon he said to her, " Didn't I tell you that through him the Temple was destroyed and through him it would be rebuilt? "

PERSONS

The Stranger
The Young Wife
Her Servant
Guryon ⎫
Tarfon ⎬ *Three Old Men*
Gamaliel ⎭
Berachiah
First Guard
Second Guard
Third Guard
First Woman
Second Woman
Third Woman
Fourth Woman
An Old Man

Men, women and children of various classes of the population.

The action takes place in the city of Birath Arba in the time of the destruction of the second Temple.

THE STRANGER

Scene

The marketplace of Birath Arba in the background, and to the right and left, shops, consisting of wooden booths placed a short distance from each other, laden with various articles: clothes, dishes, woolens. In the middle of the square rise three cedar trees. Behind the booths is visible a row of wooden dwellings with trees growing before them.

From the right of the marketplace comes the noise of a large crowd. The shopkeepers, all of them elderly people, stand in a group near the shops at the right, and look with frightened countenances in the direction of the commotion. From the houses at the rear and at the left, men, women and children begin to pour forth, agitated, terrified. The noise comes nearer; cries are heard distinctly: "Woe unto us! Woe unto us! Evil tidings have come! Woe unto us! Woe unto us!"

Enter Guryon, Tarfon *and* Gamaliel, *three snow-white old men, followed by a large crowd that presses upon the place from between the booths. The men of the group are mostly middle-aged or older; the few youths among them are cripples.*

Guryon (*in a tearful voice*). Children of Israel,

give ear to me, and prepare to hear. Zion is in the throes of death and Jerusalem is about to fall.

An Outburst of Lamentation. Woe! Woe! Woe unto us!

Guryon. A man has just passed by, a refugee from Jerusalem, and frightful is the tale he bears. Your hearts will melt like wax, and your eyes will brim over with tears.

An Outburst (*stronger than before*). Woe! Woe unto us!

Guryon. Step by step the besieged army was compelled to retreat before the Romans. They fought like lions and infuriated bulls. Hungry, exhausted, faint from lack of sleep, they yet withstood the enemy, and every step forward was dearly paid for by Roman blood. But, alas! The Romans conquered, and now there remains to our defenders only a single stronghold — the Temple. There they have locked themselves in and the Romans are laying siege to them. Woe, woe unto us! The Romans are besieging the Temple! The Romans are already before the walls of the Temple! (*Bursts into tears. The lamentation of the crowd waxes louder.*)

An Outburst. Woe unto us! Woe unto us!

Gamaliel (*tearfully*). And hunger is growing in the city. People die in the streets; they fall like flies. Folks go around like shadows, peering about for something to eat. Miriam, the daughter of Boethius, the wife of the High Priest Joshua —

Tarfon. One of the wealthiest women in Jerusalem. She used to walk from her house to the Temple upon carpets, costly carpets from Persia. I myself have held them in my hands; carpets that cost a fortune.

Gamaliel. And she was wont to use two hundred measures of wine each day — two hundred measures of wine — so you may well imagine her luxurious table! This selfsame Miriam now walks through the streets of Jerusalem and takes into her mouth the most nauseating objects she finds, stilling her hunger with whatever she can swallow. Miriam, daughter of Nicodemus —

Tarfon. Was even wealthier than Miriam, daughter of Boethius. She used to give five hundred golden pieces every day for incense in the Temple.

Gamaliel. She wanders through the streets of Jerusalem, picking up the oats that fall from horses' feed. (*His bitter weeping increases.*) Oh! The curse of the world has come upon us! Mothers kill their little children, in order to eat flesh. (*The weeping of the crowd rises to a new outburst.*)

Tarfon (*breaking suddenly into lamentation*). Woe to our heads! The Temple has surely been destroyed already, and Jerusalem has fallen!

Voices. Woe to our heads! Woe! Woe! The Temple has surely been destroyed!

Gamaliel (*bitterly*). Woe unto us! Woe unto us!

A Woman (*begins to pull her hair, with a bitter outcry*). Woe! Woe! Woe!

Guryon (*struggling with his weakness*). Silence, you fools! (*To* Tarfon). How could you speak so? You are old and grey, yet have not learned what miracles the Lord can work. Is it not a miracle that our hungry warriors are victorious over the Romans day after day, and repulse their well-fed legions? Is it not a miracle that many of the Romans, moved by the courage and the heroism of the Jews, desert their banner and their gods and come to our God and to our people? (*There is a stir.*)

VOICES. Do they? Is that really so?

GURYON. Day after day they do so. (*A stir.*)

VOICES. Lord, how almighty Thou art!

GURYON. Will He, our omnipotent Lord, permit His House to fall? How could you have spoken so, Tarfon?

TARFON. Did He not, then, allow His first Temple to be destroyed? I am afraid! I am afraid!

VOICES. Woe unto us! Woe unto us!

GURYON. May your tongue be paralyzed, Tarfon! You blaspheme the Lord, and your words serve only to encourage Satan. And I tell you that the Temple has not been destroyed. Do you imagine that God's House would be destroyed and we and the whole world would not have felt it immediately? Would not the sun have grown dark, and would not the heavens be veiled in sorrow, shedding bitter tears? Would not our hearts weep within our bosoms, and would we not know whence came the tears? And not only we, but even the creatures of the forest and the beasts of the field should be aware of it. Sin not with your speech, and shed your tears not in lamentation, but in entreaty and prayer. Let us clothe ourselves in sackcloth, cover our heads with ashes and torment our bodies with fasting. Let us beg the Lord to be merciful, to remove His heavy hand from His people, and deliver His holy kingdom. Come, let us all pass the day in weeping and in prayer. (*The crowd stirs. The lamentation breaks forth anew.*)

VOICES. Fetch sackcloth! Bring ashes!

A MAN'S VOICE (*within, to the left of the booths*). Swaddling clothes for sale! Clothes for new-born children! Swaddling clothes for sale! For new-born children! (*All eyes turn to the left.*)

GURYON. Who can that be, crying his wares so calmly, while our people are plunged in sorrow?

THE STRANGER (*enters between the two forward shops at the left, carrying a peddler's pack upon his shoulders*). That's what I call my luck. I see gathered on this marketplace the whole city of Birath Arba, so that it will be all the easier for me to find whom I seek. Tell me, dwells there not among you one Hezekiah by name, to whom was born a son on the day the Temple was destroyed, and who named his son Menahem? (*Commotion.*)

A TERRIFIED MURMURING. On the day the Temple was destroyed?

GURYON, TARFON *and* GAMALIEL (*with consternation*). On the day the Temple was destroyed?

GURYON. Has the Temple been destroyed?

THE STRANGER (*astonished*). You do not know it? Or is it not — (*firmly*). Yes, our Temple has been destroyed; the crown of our head has fallen.

VOICES OF LAMENTATION. Our Temple has been

destroyed; the crown of our head has fallen!

TARFON (*with a trembling voice*). Guryon, you see —

GURYON (*to* THE STRANGER, *in a voice choked with tears*). Do you come from Jerusalem, or from its vicinity?

THE STRANGER. I come neither from Jerusalem nor from its vicinity. Birath Arba lies midway between Jerusalem and my home.

GURYON (*raises his eyes, filled with surprise, to* THE STRANGER). And still you already know what we have not yet learned. Did you meet upon the road people from Jerusalem or from its vicinity?

THE STRANGER. I met nobody upon my way. The roads now are abandoned, deserted, without a traveler. Only, at frequent intervals, hordes of Roman soldiers, in high spirits, march by. And they are dangerous because they kill or take prisoner every Jew they encounter. Through forests and night I stole hither, and the journey which ordinarily would have taken me two days, consumed ten.

GURYON. You come not from Jerusalem, and have met nobody on the way, yet you say —

THE STRANGER. And yet I tell you that the Temple has been destroyed, and that the same day there was born Menahem, who will console us in our misfortune and deliver us from our enemies. And that Menahem is among you in Birath Arba. (*Commotion.*)

MURMURING AMONG THE PEOPLE. A prophet? — Perhaps a false prophet! — Yes, a false prophet!

GURYON (*sternly*). Who are you that you know things which you have neither seen nor heard? Has the Lord sent you a token? Has He revealed it to you in a dream?

THE STRANGER. Your mouth has spoken it. God has revealed it to me through a token.

MURMURING. A prophet! — A false prophet!

GURYON. Speak, and let us know whether to believe you. Who are you, tell us, and how did the Lord reveal Himself to you?

THE STRANGER. I will tell you straightway, but first let me sit down and moisten my parched throat. (*Lowers his pack, sits down upon the earth, takes a drink of water from his skin-bottle, and a bite of carob.*) I was a tiller of the soil in a village far in Galilee, and dearer than all else to me was my little piece of earth. When war with the Romans broke out, I was the only able-bodied man left in my village with my oxen, and did not go to help our people and our country.

A CRIPPLE (*in the front line of the crowd*). He confesses that without blushing for shame!

THE STRANGER. Hear me further. It was no easy matter for me to remain behind. I waged a bitter battle in my bosom. On one side my people called me, on the other, my beloved earth, until the earth drew me to itself. To my people I am but a lone individual, I said to myself, but to my earth I am all. So I remained with my earth. Around and around our land was devastated. City after city and district after district was captured by the Romans, until at last they beleaguered Jerusalem and more than ever our people needed its sturdy sons. And all this I knew, yet I did not stir from my place. I was ashamed to look to right or to left, yet continued to walk behind my oxen. I was as if grown into my earth, unable to uproot myself from it.

GURYON (*hard*). Be brief. We wish to know the Lord's token.

THE STRANGER (*arising*). I'll tell it directly. Ten days ago I was in the field with my oxen. Suddenly they became so restless, and began to cry with such strange sounds, as if something had frightened them. I looked in every direction, under my oxen and above, and beheld nothing that could have given them fright. And since they continued to cry, I raised my staff and beat them, saying to them, "Why do you cry so, you foolish oxen!" And of a sudden there appears before me an old, old man, with snow-white hair and snow-white beard, and dressed like an Arabian. And he says to me, "Beat not your oxen. Rather unyoke them and cast aside your work, for in this moment the Temple has been destroyed." I cried out in terror, and with trembling heart and quivering hands I did as he bade me. But the oxen began to cry anew. This time the sounds they made seemed as if filled with joy. And the old man spoke again to me. "Yoke your oxen," he said, "and return to your labors, for in this moment there has been born the Messiah who will deliver the Jews from their enemies and rebuild the Temple." (*Becoming excited.*) And something stirred within me, and I asked the old man what was the name of the new-born child. And he replied, "Menahem is his name." And his father's name? "Hezekiah," he answered. Where does he live? And he responded, "In Birath Arba you will find Menahem's mother." (*Commotion.*)

MURMURING OF VOICES. Did you hear? Did you hear? Hezekiah — Menahem —

THE STRANGER. And as soon as he had spoken this, he vanished before my very eyes, and I knew that God had sent him to me. (*His excitement grows.*) At first I was overwhelmed with terror, and trembling in every limb I looked about me, and it seemed as if someone were beside me, crowding against me. I wanted to return to my work, but could not. And suddenly my eyes became two springs, and tears began to flow in two streams. And I threw myself down upon the earth and wept bitterly. And when the tears came no longer, a thought filled my head and my heart. Why had God chosen me to receive such a revelation? And it seemed to me as if someone at once answered from beside me, "You earth-worm, bound to the soil, the Lord wishes to punish you for your indifference to your people's sorrows, for your heart of stone which the misfortunes of your Nation have failed to move!" I looked around, but saw no one near. It was as if God had spoken to me, and again the great terror descended upon me, and I feared to look to right, to left. And there I sat with eyes closed, and my great terror within me, and with head and heart sought to discover what punishment God had here chosen for me. And suddenly a dark feeling filled me, sending a shudder through my whole body. Everything began to turn before my eyes, and I seemed to hear a voice speaking to me: "You earth-worm, bound to the soil, you did not care to help your people in its war for freedom, and did not care to stand up for its holy Temple. Go and seek out its redeemer and the builder of its future Temple, and be unto him an eternal vassal." And filled with terror, I asked myself, if God wishes this of me, why has His messenger not told it to me? And I sank into meditation, seeking a reply, and waiting for a token from God. And again it seemed as if someone spoke beside me. "God gave you the choice before and gives it to you now. Before, you chose the wrong; now choose the right." And with wildly beating heart I arose from the earth, drove my oxen into the city, sold them together with the yoke, and for the money I received I bought linen for swaddling clothes, so that I might cry my wares in Birath Arba, and ask whatever woman came to me what was her husband's name and when her child was born. But now you are all gathered here —

GURYON. And is that your whole story? What proof will you show us, that we may believe you?

THE STRANGER. Is it not proof enough that I come to you from afar and tell you that on the selfsame day on which the Temple was destroyed there was born our redeemer, and that he is here among you?

GURYON. This happened ten days ago, you say? And he is named Menahem? And his father Hezekiah? (*To the populace.*) Does any of you know a Hezekiah, to whom ten days ago was born a son whom he named Menahem?

MURMURING. Do you know such a one? Do you know Hezekiah?

VOICE (*from the back of the crowd*). My name is Hezekiah, but no child has been born to me in the last twelve years.

ANOTHER VOICE (*from the side*). There is a Hezekiah, son of Halphi, but he has been a widower for these four years.

A WOMAN'S VOICE. I have not heard of a child being born among us for a month. And I am a midwife.

GURYON (*to* THE STRANGER). Do you hear? Your proof is no proof at all.

MURMURING. His proof is no proof at all! A false proof! A false prophet!

THE STRANGER. That you do not know is surely no proof against me, and you shall see that I will find here the mother of Menahem.

GURYON. Now I will tell you who you are. You are a fool and a false prophet —

VOICES. A false prophet! A false prophet!

GURYON. You are one of those who are overrunning our land in these days.

TARFON. You are a downright impostor who is looking only to make good profits from his children's linens. But we have no need here of your swaddling clothes. There are places to buy them, without you. I have plenty of them in my own shop.

Gamaliel. You are a liar who little cares that with his falsehoods he can make his hearers' hearts stop beating and take away all desire to eat or drink.

Guryon. You are a sinner and a blasphemer who utters evil words to weaken the faith of believers in God.

Tarfon. He wants to cry his wares all the louder, so he invents a likely tale. You deserve to be beaten, you impostor!

Voices. Beat him! Stone him! Stone him! (*The circle about* The Stranger *becomes narrower, and hands are raised against him.*)

The Stranger. Hold! (*The din subsides.*) Give me but three days' time, and if within those three days I do not discover the child Menahem, or you learn that the Temple has not been destroyed, then you may stone me. But should you learn within those three days that the Temple has been destroyed as I have told you, and if I do not within that time discover the child Menahem, then allow me to remain in your city and wait, for I am sure that I shall find him.

Guryon. Let it be as you say. And more. We will at once send out messengers upon the various roads to Jerusalem to learn how matters stand there, and you shall remain here until they return. And if they bring back reports that show you to have lied, we will punish you as a false prophet deserves to be punished. But if the reports show you to have told the truth, and the Temple is really destroyed, you may remain here as long as you please, and we shall all wait to see what time will bring forth for you. Our meeting-house stands open to you. There you will sleep at night and find your rest by day.

THE STRANGER. My profuse thanks. But the sky over my head has always been roof enough for me. I shall remain here upon the marketplace and cry my wares until Menahem's mother comes to me.

TARFON. Do not believe him. He will sell out his wares and then he will leave to spread his lies broadcast and utter blasphemy.

THE STRANGER. I will sell nothing to any woman.

GAMALIEL. We shall have to watch him, lest he run away.

GURYON. Leave everything to me. All will be right. (*Turns to several of the bystanders.*) You, Berachiah, and you, and you, and you, off at once upon the roads that lead to Jerusalem. Should you meet anyone coming from Jerusalem, very well indeed. Then you can learn from him at once how matters stand there. But be sure to question him thoroughly, and not believe his very first words. For who knows who the person may be. Better wait to meet a second and a third, and if they all tell the same story, you may then believe. In that case, bring us the news just as it is; good or bad, bring it to us as fast as your feet can carry you. But should you encounter nobody — for the roads are deserted and desolate — then press on to Jerusalem, steal in behind the Roman lines, if that be necessary, make your way into the city and learn everything. And bring us the news as fast as possible.

BERACHIAH. Do you not think that your last suggestion is a very dangerous one?

GURYON. That I know quite well, my friend. But I did not know that in Birath Arba there were grown-up men who would decline a mission because it was dangerous.

VOICES. Well spoken, Guryon!

BERACHIAH. Very well. We leave at once. (BERACHIAH *and the three other men leave, followed by several women and children, who accompany them out, to the right. The women dry their eyes.*)

GURYON (*to three other men in the crowd*). And you three remain here on guard over the stranger. See to it that he does not squirm out of his well-merited punishment.

ONE OF THE THREE. We will guard him well.

GURYON. And let all the rest of us go into the meeting-house to pass the time in prayer and in fasting, garbed in sackcloth and with ashes upon our heads. (*Leaves toward the left, followed by* TARFON *and* GAMALIEL *and then the crowd. The shopkeepers hurriedly pack their wares and close their shops, hastening after the crowd. There remain upon the stage only* THE STRANGER, THE THREE GUARDS *and some women from nearby houses. A few of the latter have their children with them. They stand in groups near the shops and stare at* THE STRANGER.)

THE STRANGER (*sits down, opens his pack and looks at the linens, speaking as if to himself*). Menahem, son of Hezekiah — Menahem, son of Hezekiah —

FIRST GUARD. Repeat it well, repeat it well, so that you shall not forget your lie.

SECOND GUARD. That will do him no good. He will not carry his lie out of this city, anyway.

THIRD GUARD. He will be buried under a heap of stones, together with his lie.

THE STRANGER (*arises and calls*). Swaddling clothes for sale! Linens for new-born children! Swaddling clothes! Linens for new-born children!

FIRST GUARD. Cry louder! Your Hezekiah's wife is deaf in one of her feet and lame in an ear.

SECOND GUARD. Look out! Look out! She'll fall right down on your head.

THE STRANGER. Swaddling clothes for sale! Linens for new-born children!

THIRD GUARD. He shouts and shouts, and doesn't become hoarse. Maybe we have a madman on our hands!

A WOMAN (*approaches the stranger's pack*). We may as well look at his wares meanwhile. (*Several other women draw near and begin to examine the linens.*)

FIRST WOMAN. It is good linen.

SECOND WOMAN. Excellent.

THIRD WOMAN. Tarfon's cloth is not half so good.

FOURTH WOMAN. And Gamla's is much worse.

FIRST WOMAN. I have a good mind to buy some. How much is it by the ell?

THE STRANGER. Do not be foolish, woman. If your husband's name is not Hezekiah, and your son's Menahem, then you can get no goods from me.

FIRST WOMAN. So you are really afraid of the guards? That is all right. They will close their eyes and pretend not to see.

SECOND WOMAN. And if my child is a girl, and is named Tamar, is she not entitled to some of your good linen?

THIRD WOMAN. And if my son's name is Nahmen, he surely is entitled to some? How far is it from Nahmen to Menahem?

FIRST WOMAN. How much does an ell cost? You may tell us, at least? (*The Stranger closes his pack.*)

FOURTH WOMAN. See, he closes his bundle and does not even look at us.

FIRST GUARD. Alas, what a defeat! Our most beautiful women have besieged a man and could not capture him.

FIRST WOMAN. If only you weren't here.

FIRST GUARD. What will you give me if I shut my eyes?

SECOND GUARD. And I want a share.

FIRST GUARD. Her bed is too small for three.

THIRD GUARD. You shouldn't talk like that when our people are gathered in prayer and tears.

THIRD WOMAN. That is man's way: amid the

greatest misfortunes he never forgets his lust. Even at the point of slaughter, the cock pursues the hen.

THE STRANGER. Swaddling clothes for sale! Linens for new-born children!

FOURTH WOMAN. Why do you shout your wares like that? We are not deaf. Open your pack.

THE STRANGER. I do not sell to you. You already know that.

(*A young wife enters. Her clothes show that she has made a long journey on foot. She comes in at the right background, from between two shops, and stands, unobserved.*)

FIRST WOMAN. See, he really believes that we are dying to purchase his goods!

SECOND WOMAN. It is not at all so good as it seemed to be upon first inspection. It is not strong.

THIRD WOMAN. It would fall to pieces at the first washing. (*The women notice the newcomer, and look at her in surprise.*)

FIRST WOMAN (*to the Second*). Who is that standing there?

SECOND WOMAN. She is unknown to me.

THIRD WOMAN. I have never seen her, either.

FOURTH WOMAN. I could swear she is a stranger.

FIRST WOMAN. From her clothes it looks as if she had just arrived.

(*The Stranger notices the newcomer.* THE YOUNG WIFE *becomes aware that she is being closely scrutinized and steps back several paces in great embarrassment.*)

First Guard. Whom are you seeking here, my beauty?

The Stranger. Come closer, do. Why do you stand aloof? You may also inspect my wares.

(The Young Wife *approaches, hesitantly, blushing deeply with embarrassment. The other women again draw near to the* Stranger.)

First Woman. Inspect, and no more. For he will not sell you his goods.

The Young Wife (*in scarcely audible tones*). I expected it. Nor is my heart upon buying.

The Stranger. What was it you expected?

The Young Wife. That you would refuse to sell me your wares. My child of misfortune deserves it, too.

First Woman. Your child of misfortune?

The Young Wife (*with tears*). Yes, my child is a child of misfortune. It is —

First Guard. What ails your child? Speak clearly.

The Young Wife (*weeping*). It was born to me on the day our Temple was destroyed! (*Intense commotion; exclamations of great astonishment.*)

The Stranger. Ha! What was that you said?

The Young Wife. I knew that you would all be surprised. My child and I deserve to be scorned.

First Guard (*in great agitation*). Where do you come from? Speak!

The Young Wife. From Jerusalem.

The Stranger. When was your child born? Tell us once more.

THE YOUNG WIFE. You heard me. I cannot bring it to my lips again.

SECOND GUARD. How long — how long ago did this happen?

THE YOUNG WIFE. Surely you must know. Ten days ago. (*A stir, and renewed exclamations of amazement.*)

THE STRANGER. What is the name of your child?

THE YOUNG WIFE. My child of misfortune bears a false name. His father wished it so. His name is Menahem. (*The commotion grows. The bystanders recoil in fear from the Stranger and the Young Wife.*)

THE STRANGER (*breathlessly*). Ah! And what is your husband's name?

THE YOUNG WIFE. Why do you shout so? (*Looks at him closely and throws herself impetuously upon him.*) Then you know my husband, perhaps? Do you know me? Do you know, perhaps, what has become of my husband? Have you some terrible news to tell me? I see it in your eyes. You are frightened, you are confused. (*Hysterically.*) Tell me! Have the Romans slain him? Have they sold him into slavery? Tell me, where! Tell me, to whom! (*Tearing her hair madly.*) My Hezekiah! My Hezekiah! (*General consternation.*)

THE STRANGER. Oh! (*He clutches his heart and his head and rubs his eyes as if struggling against a feeling of faintness. Several of the women seize their children and run off in hysterical fright.*)

First Guard (*to the* Second Guard). Run at once to fetch Guryon, Tarfon and Gamaliel. Tell them what you have heard, and bid them to come here directly. (Second Guard *runs off to the left.*)

The Stranger (*regains his composure and speaks in a quiet voice*). Calm yourself. I know neither you nor your husband. I bring no news of him. Tell me, rather — (*Cries out exultantly.*) Tell me, rather, where is your son? Where have you left your Menahem?

The Young Wife (*scarcely able to speak*). I left him in a house on the outskirts of the city. (*Brokenly.*) Why do you persist in questioning me about my child of misfortune?

The Stranger. Silence, woman! You know not what you speak. Your son is not a child of misfortune, but a child of happiness and consolation. He is a Menahem, a "consoler" of our people. On the day of his birth the Temple was destroyed and our people defeated, but he will rebuild our Temple and will lead our people to new victories.

The Young Wife. What are you talking about? Are you trying to console me? Or are you mocking an unhappy woman?

The Stranger. Come, lead me to your son. God has appointed me His vassal and He sent me hither from afar, to find him here. Come! You will hear everything. Come, lead me to your son! Upon my arms I will carry him and watch over him, even as the most faithful nurse. Come, quickly!

First Guard. Halt! You must not leave this

spot! I see it all now. This is a plot. This woman is in league with you and wants to save you from our hands.

THE STRANGER. You blasphemer, you evil-tongued wretch, you carrion-mouth, how dare you now speak so? How can you hold me back from that to which God has appointed me?

FIRST GUARD. Perhaps I am wrong. But you shall not leave. We were placed here to guard you and we will not release you. You yourself promised to remain here in the market-place. Keep your pledge.

THE STRANGER. Yes, I promised it: until she should come — the mother of Menahem.

FIRST GUARD. You must wait until Guryon returns.

THE STRANGER. Jew, you are sinning now against your Messiah.

FIRST GUARD. I am doing my duty.

THE STRANGER. Then I must wait, and that is a grievous sin.

THE YOUNG WIFE. I understand nothing of what you two are saying.

THE STRANGER. You will understand later. God appointed me to come hither and seek you out, because your son was born to be our Messiah.

THE YOUNG WIFE. The child of misfortune?

THE STRANGER. Name him not so, I have already told you. And how come you, pray, to call him thus? (*The women draw closer and surround the* YOUNG WIFE *and the* STRANGER.)

The Young Wife. How else could he be called, when he was born on such a day? Oh, how I prayed not to have him on that day! I entreated God not to open my womb, that my child should not have to go through life with the consciousness that on the day of his birth his people was visited with the most terrible and grievous of disasters — that he should not be to me as an eternal tombstone over the grave of my nation and its faith. And when God did not give ear to me, and the pangs of my labor increased, I wished to oppose the Lord and work my own will. I bit my lips and held in my breath. I wanted to keep my child in my womb. And when the pains grew stronger and I gasped for air, losing the strength of my will — and when I saw that the child would be born despite all, I prayed to God that it be born dead. "Lord," I cried, "this will be your greatest mercy. Lord," I wept, "how shall I be able to rejoice in my child, when my whole people is blind with tears and plunged in defeat?" And I restrained my cries of anguish and prayed to God. "Lord, my husband has gone off to wage war for your Sacred House and for the freedom of your chosen people. He was not held back by his deep love for me or by his joyous expectation of the child under my breast. And I, too, choked back my tears and prepared him for war, and if I had not had the child under my breast, I would not have let him depart alone, but would have marched along with him and fought side by side with him against your enemies and together with your noble sons. You know my heart, and know that I would have done so. Now show me your mercy, and let me not yet bear my child, or let it be born dead." But God deserted His chosen people, and abandoned me, too. I gave birth to the child, and, as you see, he was born alive.

THE STRANGER. That was the third hour after mid-day?

THE YOUNG WIFE. You know that, too? Yes, it was the third hour after mid-day. The last walls of the Temple had collapsed in the flames and the last heroes were slain and in that selfsame moment my son's cries filled the house. How happy should I have been, had I heard his first cries at any other time. But all I could do then was weep, and I wept long and bitterly, and from the street there came into my home the wailing of our people. (*Bursts into tears.*)

THE STRANGER. Weep not. You spoil your milk.

THE YOUNG WIFE. My milk — my milk is as bitter as gall. And I grudge him every drop. As soon as he was born I became angry with God. I raised my hand against Heaven, and cried, "God, you desired him to live, then give him nourishment, for I will not suckle him." I turned away and did not even wish to see him. But when he began to cry louder and louder, I, too, burst into tears and took him to my breast — with my eyes closed, so as not to see him. (*From the left comes the mingling of many voices.*)

THE STRANGER. Here they come. Oh, I shall soon behold your son! (GURYON, TARFON, GAMA-

LIEL *and the* SECOND GUARD *enter, followed by the populace, all in sackcloth and ashes.*)

GURYON. Where is the woman? Where is she? (*The women separate.* GURYON *approaches the* YOUNG WIFE.) Are you the woman from Jerusalem?

THE YOUNG WIFE. I am the woman.

GURYON. And you say that the Temple has fallen?

THE YOUNG WIFE (*her eyes wide open with surprise*). And you have not yet heard of it?

GURYON. We have not heard of it, nor do we know it now.

THE YOUNG WIFE (*with tears*). It happened ten days ago. At the third hour after mid-day its last walls crumbled in.

VOICES. Hear! Hear! Tremble ye heavens! (*Wailing.*)

GURYON. Whither go you now, and what seek you here?

THE YOUNG WIFE. I seek my husband. He was in the army against the Romans, under Eleazer, and was captured. I have been informed that he is now in Syria. Thither I am journeying; I am merely passing through this city.

GURYON. Are you telling us the truth? Will you swear to your words? (*There is a disturbance at the right.*)

BERACHIAH, *and* ONE OF THE MESSENGERS (*come running in, their clothes torn*). Woe unto us! Woe unto us! The Temple has fallen! Fallen! Fallen!

(*The* YOUNG WIFE *bursts into tears; the other women do likewise.*)

GURYON. When did this happen?

BERACHIAH. Precisely as the Stranger related, ten days ago.

GURYON. How did you learn of this?

BERACHIAH. As soon as we had struck the road to Hebron, we came upon a horde of Jews who were making their way thence to Gilead, and they told us the woeful tidings with tears in their eyes and with a wringing of hands.

THE STRANGER. Now lead me to your son! Come all, follow me! Shed tears for what has been lost, but rejoice in what is to come. A son has been born unto her, and he is called Menahem, and he will be to us a consoler and a redeemer, a builder and a reconstructor! Follow me! Come, behold the child! Come, fortunate woman, lead us to your child — your child of good fortune, your child of redemption! (*There is a stir in the background. The* SERVANT *and the* OLD MAN *elbow their way to the* YOUNG WIFE).

THE SERVANT (*falls wailing upon her knees before the* YOUNG WIFE). Kill me! Woe!

THE YOUNG WIFE. What has happened?

THE SERVANT. Kill me! Put me to death! Your child is no more!

THE YOUNG WIFE (*in terror*). My child is dead?

THE STRANGER. Menahem is dead?

MURMURING AMONG THE PEOPLE (*with accents of despair*). Dead?

The Servant (*struggling for breath between her sobs*). No. Not dead!

The Stranger (*enlightened*). Oh!

Murmuring Among the People. Not dead!

The Young Wife. Then what has befallen him?

The Servant. Hear me out. You left me with your child outside, before the house, until you should return with the swaddling clothes; and I lay the child down before me and began to sew his little shirt. Suddenly it became dark, just like before a storm — I had not noticed how the darkness came upon us — and a great wind arose. I leaned over to the child, about to take it into my arms and carry it indoors: suddenly I was blown about by the wind, my eyes were filled with sand — and I felt as if someone tore the child from my grasp. And when I opened my eyes it was light again, but I did not see the child. I looked around, began to seek, but could not find him. I raised an alarm, the people came out of their houses, I told them the misfortune, they helped me seek, and we sought far and wide, but could not find him. They are here with me, they can bear witness that I tell no lie.

The Old Man (*at her side*). She speaks the pure truth. I happened to be standing at the window, and it was just as if I saw the wind raise the child aloft and bear it away.

The Young Wife. My child!

The Servant. Put me to death if I am guilty!

The Young Wife. Arise, you are not guilty. Such is my child's fate.

VOICES. Why do we stand here? Let us run to seek the child. (THE STRANGER *appears to awaken.*)

GURYON. What would you have? (THE STRANGER *relapses into revery.*)

THE YOUNG WIFE (*through her tears*). Did I not tell you that he was a child of misfortune?

THE STRANGER (*uttering his words with deliberation, his gaze fixed upon the distance*). Name him not so. He is no child of misfortune, I have told you. On the day of his birth the Temple was destroyed, but he was born to build us a new one. I go to seek him. God has imposed this task upon me. I see it clearly. (*Of a sudden he becomes old, and his hair and beard turn white.*)

VOICES. See how he looks! See how he looks!

GURYON (*recoils in terror*). And *him* we called liar and sinner?

THE STRANGER. Sinner, yes. I have committed the most evil of sins. I did not care to fight for the freedom of my people. Now God's terrible punishment descends upon me. I shall have to wander over the length and breadth of the earth. I see it. And long, long shall I have to seek. I feel it. I do what I must. (*Places the peddler's pack on his shoulders.*) I do what I must. (*With uplifted arms he leaves in the direction of the right.*)

THE YOUNG WIFE (*falls prostrate*). My child! (*The bystanders sink to their knees.*)

CURTAIN